FRUIT AND VEGGIES 101
THE WINTER HARVEST

GARDENING GUIDE ON HOW TO GROW THE FRESHEST & RIPEST WINTER VEGETABLES (PERFECT FOR BEGINNERS)

GREEN ROOTS

Fruit and Veggies 101

THE WINTER HARVEST

Gardening Guide On How To Grow The Freshest & Ripest Winter Vegetables

(Perfect For Beginners)

GREEN ROOTS

CONTENTS

A SPECIAL GIFT TO OUR READERS

Included with your purchase of this book is our list of "27 horticulture Myths Debunked"
This list will provide and aid you as a new (or soon-to-be) gardener by actively informing you of the myths and irrelevant practices to avoid during your gardening journey.

Visit the link below to let us know which email address to deliver to

www.gardengreenroots.com

INTRODUCTION

It's a common assumption that gardening's only benefits are its organic, cost-effective, and convenient results. While these are certainly among the greatest, gardening has much more to give than just physical produce. We are talking about how gardening is used to aid your physical, mental, and emotional well-being.

These additional benefits are commonly overlooked and are not given enough credit when it comes to the advantages of gardening. Understanding that improving your well-being is ultimately improving the quality of your vegetable crops.

It takes discipline, passion, love and a load more personal trait to consistently wake up each day and care for your vegetable plants. Where and how were these personal traits developed? Whether you were aware or not; these traits are a result of well-being being prioritised. By understanding this you can truly value and appreciate the significance of gardening.

"Gardening is not just a hobby, but a way of life" - **(Green Roots 2022)**

Spending as little as 10 minutes in the garden can help lower your blood pressure and heart rate while boosting your mood, shifting your mind-set from negative to positive. Being in the garden has shown to reduce stress, anxiety, depression and also increases overall energy levels.

These benefits are critical for maintaining one's well-being, as being in nature can help you feel more connected to the world around you,; increasing your sense of self-efficacy. So the next time you're feeling stressed or down, try heading outside for a little dose of nature; you might be surprised at how much it can help.

RECLAIM AND REVITALIZE YOUR WELL-BEING WITH GARDENING

It's no secret that life can be challenging. From work and family to managing our finances, there's a lot on our plates, and sometimes it can all feel too much. You are not alone! We can personally relate to this life experience, and many others can as well. It is far from something to be ashamed of, as it's simply the journey of life, and that's where gardening comes in.

Gardening is more than just a hobby - it's a way to reclaim and revitalize your well-being. When working with your hands in the dirt, all your stress and worries seem to fade away. For those few moments, you're entirely focused on the task at hand, and nothing else matters.

Twenty years of collective gardening experience has shown us how powerful the practice can be. We've seen individuals' lives transformed and changed by learning to plant for themselves. So in situations where you feel unproductive, lonely or not in the best of spaces mentally, we can assure you that learning how to plant, cultivate and grow vegetables from almost nothing but a seed, to full of nutrients and tasty vegetables will surely drive those feelings away.

I'm sure you've heard or seen the phrase "hiding in plain sight"; we believe this phrase perfectly describes one of the most underrated or even underestimated methods for prioritizing and caring for your well-being, and this is through the art of gardening.

Few things are as satisfying as biting into a sandwich made with fresh and crunchy lettuces that you grew or enjoying a salad made entirely of vegetables you planted and tended with your own two hands.

Growing your vegetables has many benefits. For one, you can be sure of the food quality since you know the conditions they grew in. This means that you can avoid pesticides and other chemicals and have more control over the size and shape of your vegetables and when they are harvested.

It is generally known that home-grown vegetables are usually fresher and tastier than those bought from a store. So it's an all-round win growing your vegetables and gaining that sense of accomplishment that comes from watching your plants grow and flourish.

Reclaiming and revitalizing your well-being with gardening is essentially reclaiming control over your health and lifestyle. Simply choosing where and what type of vegetables to grow based on your lifestyle and preferences is a catalyst in creating and implementing that sense of control in one's life.

What happens next is that this rejuvenated sense of control transplants into other areas of one's lifestyle. Hence, we can confidently say, *"We've seen individual's lives transformed and changed by learning to plant for themselves"*.

WHAT YOU CAN EXPECT TO LEARN

In this book, you will learn all there is to know about gardening for winter vegetables. This comprehensive yet beginner-friend guide provides direct and actionable step-by-step guidance on how to grow the freshest and ripest winter vegetables. You will learn to choose what gardening methods and locations best suit your growing objectives.

Advise on identifying and preparing your soil; decide what vegetable is ideal for your goals; then learn how to sow and plant your desired vegetables.

The vegetables you will learn to plant and grow successfully are onions, peas, Brussels sprouts, garlic, winter herbs (Rosemary, Oregano and Thyme), broccoli and lettuces. In each chapter, we will detail the preferred sowing techniques, watering, fertilization, growing stages, how to protect your crops, maintain your crops, harvesting and finally, storing and saving seeds for future cultivation.

Whether a beginner or an experienced gardener, this book will provide you with all the information you need to grow healthy and delicious winter vegetables.

WHY THIS BOOK IS EXACTLY WHAT YOU NEED

You may be wondering if this is the right book to help you get started in the world of vegetable gardening. Well, we're pleased to say that we have injected 20 years of collective gardening knowledge and experience into this book. Methods and practise that will confidently produce fresh and ripe vegetables season after season.

There are a lot of myths and misconceptions surrounding gardening, such as you need a specific set of tools (some of which are expensive), a lot of space that you might not have, and special gardening skills are required to grow wholesome and nutritious vegetables. In addition to debunking these myths, we'll show you how to maximize the area and gardening equipment you may already have.

Don't worry if you lack a gardener's unique and talented hands; successful gardeners are formed through learning, guidance and application, rather than born with these skills. You took the first steps to becoming a successful gardener, and you will achieve great results with the knowledge we have shared in this book.

You may already have a vegetable garden but are frustrated because it isn't turning out as expected. Maybe you want to start a vegetable garden but don't know where to start and feel overwhelmed. We have not only worked on our own vegetable gardens over the years, but we have also assisted others in creating and successfully maintaining their own. You're in good hands. This book will help you along your gardening journey; so let the adventure begin!

CHAPTER 1
YOUR GROWING SPACE: PREPARATIONS AND TECHNIQUES

Remember how we mentioned several myths and misconceptions surrounding growing a vegetable garden? The same can be said about myths about where one should plant their garden. As your interest in vegetable gardening has grown, we're sure you've discovered more than a few gardening myths about where and how to grow your vegetables.

Some people believe vegetables should only be grown in full sun, while others think they will do just fine in partial shade. Some are adamant that raised bed is the best practice, while others would say otherwise.

The truth is that each vegetable has different and specific requirements for it to thrive. Understanding this and how you can create the optimum environment before planting is essential or it could all be for nothing. So before we get into planting and growing our winter vegetables, this chapter will dive into the importance and steps of selecting a suitable growing space, while understanding the significance of identifying your garden soil and how to treat it. Your soil is essential to the well-being of your plants, so ensuring they have the proper nutrients and conditions will ensure they grow strong and healthy.

CHOOSE WHERE YOUR GARDEN WILL GROW

Before starting a garden, it is crucial to choose the location carefully. You will need to inspect your home and yard for what will work best for you. That's because your living environment and home will likely dictate the kind of garden you settle on.

The location will determine the type of vegetable that can be grown, the amount of sunlight, water, and the level of upkeep required. It is also essential to consider the size of the area to be planted. A small vegetable garden can be quickly tended by hand, while a larger one may require machinery.

When choosing a location for your garden, there are several factors to consider. First, you must decide whether you need a sunny or a shaded garden. Sun gardens require at least six hours of direct sunlight daily, while shade gardens can be as little as three hours.

To determine what location best suits your goals, we advise you to study when the sun rises, how much direct sunlight it gets, and when the sun falls at different garden spots for a few days. Secondly, you will need to consider the soil type; however, we'll root deeper into this in the following chapters.

Once your location is chosen, it's time to decide on the type of garden to grow. Most people not well versed in vegetable gardening only think of planting in the ground; however, there is more than one way to go about it.

Vegetable gardens can be grown in three ways: in-ground, which is the conventional method, in containers, or raised beds.

Each of these might or might not be suitable for your garden or the vegetables you want to grow, so we'll address the advantages and disadvantages of each type to help guide you to a decision best suited for your circumstance and goals.

IN-GROUND GARDEN

A traditional in-ground garden is a garden dug into the ground instead of being built above it. In-ground gardens are the most common type of garden and can be found in both urban and rural areas.

Typically, in-ground gardens are rectangular; they are divided into sections by pathways where the size of an in-ground garden can vary greatly. Your in-ground garden will need a good amount of sun exposure; as a result, ensure the area you choose to use has good sunlight.

As previously mentioned, you can do this by monitoring the area you plan to use. One advantage of traditional gardening is utilizing the naturally occurring minerals in the soil. You could save money, as purchasing additional fertilizers may not be required.

Advantages of In-Ground Gardening

- You won't need to spend too much time setting it up or constructing it.
- You will have more space.
- Vegetable roots have enough space to grow as needed.
- It will cost less money to set it up.
- You can grow a large variety of vegetables.

Disadvantage of In-Ground Gardening

- The soil may get too bulky and dense, causing slow water drainage.
- There is a chance of possible slowed plant growth due to soil compaction.
- If soil quality is terrible, it may require a lot of investment to create healthy soil.
- Possible weed and insect infestations, such as worms, may occur.
- Soil quality can be challenging to control.

CONTAINER GARDEN

A container garden is a type of gardening done in containers instead of planting directly in the ground. Container gardens are often seen as an alternative to traditional gardening, as they offer several advantages.

For one, they can be placed almost anywhere, making them ideal for small spaces. They also require less maintenance than a traditional garden, as there is no need to weed or till the soil. In addition, container gardens can be moved easily indoors during cold weather.

As a result, they offer a versatile and convenient option for those who want to enjoy the benefits of gardening without the hassle.

Advantages Of Container Gardening

- You can buy good and treated soil ready to use for containers.
- It's easy to set up.
- Containers can be movable in most cases.
- Containers can also be moved around to access adequate sunlight.
- There's virtually no weed infestation.
- There are fewer chances of soil compaction.
- A great option for easy water drainage.
- You can control the quality of your soil.

Disadvantage of Container Gardening

- It takes a decent financial investment to start.
- Roots can be compressed with little space to grow.
- Roots can rot if not properly cared for.

RAISED BED GARDEN

A raised bed garden is a type of garden where the soil is raised above the ground. This can be done by constructing raised sides out of wood, bricks, or stones.

The sides are typically about 12 inches high, making it easy to reach the plants without bending down. Raised bed gardens have several advantages over traditional gardens.

First, they allow for better drainage, which is vital in areas with a lot of rainfall. Second, the soil in a raised bed warms up more quickly in the spring, giving plants a head start on the growing season.

Finally, raised beds can be used to create a more controlled environment for sensitive plants. By choosing suitable materials and carefully monitoring the amount of sunlight and water the plants receive, gardeners can create an ideal environment for their plants to thrive.

Advantages Of Raised Bed Gardening

- With pre-made raised beds, it can be easy to set up.
- There's virtually no weed infestation.
- There are fewer chances of soil compaction.
- A great option for easy water drainage.
- You can control the quality of your soil.
- Suitable for those with physical limitations.
- Suitable for people with back problems.

Disadvantage Of Raised Bed Gardening

- It can be time-consuming and tedious to set up if the raised beds are a DIY project.
- There are financial expenses to start or set up.
- They can't be moved around like containers.

You can also create a hybrid or combination of the three gardens if you cannot decide which one to use.

BEGINNER ESSENTIALS TOOLS AND EQUIPMENT

Now that you've decided what kind of garden you want to start, we'll go over the tools you'll need to create and maintain a garden properly. With so many gardening tools on the market, it's easy to become confused and unsure what to buy.

However, we will make it very simple for you because the truth is that you don't need much to begin with; additionally, some are not required to grow a successful vegetable garden.

As a beginner, gardening can be intimidating, so we'll save you time and trouble by sharing what you need.

Pruning Shears

Garden pruning shears, also called hand pruners or secateurs, are essential tools gardeners use. These small, handheld tools are used for various tasks, including harvesting crops, trimming foliage, and cutting back small branches.

The blades of pruning shears are designed to stay sharp through years of use, and the handles are usually made from comfortable materials like wood or plastic. Many gardeners keep a pair of pruning shears in their gardening toolkit to quickly and efficiently take care of small tasks as they arise.

The advantage of purchasing this tool earlier in your journey is that you probably won't need to buy another one for a while.

Garden Rake

Garden rakes come in various shapes and sizes, but they all serve the same primary purpose: to help gather, level, and smooth out the soil. Whether preparing a bed for planting or leveling an existing garden, a rake is essential.

There are several different types of garden rakes available, each designed for specific tasks. Leaf rakes are typically lightweight and have wide tines spaced far apart. This design helps them to efficiently gather leaves and other debris without damaging delicate plants.

Garden rakes with shorter tines closer together are ideal for leveling soil and removing stones or other small debris. And finally, there are heavy-duty rakes with long, thick tines that are perfect for breaking up hard-packed grounds.

Garden Hand Trowel

A hand trowel is a small gardening tool used for various tasks, such as digging, transplanting, and aerating soil. The trowel has a long, slender handle and a small, scoop-shaped blade.

The blade is usually made of metal or plastic, and the handle is generally made of wood or plastic. A trowel is an essential tool for any gardener, as it can be used for various tasks.

For example, the trowel can dig holes for planting, transplant seedlings or young plants, and aerate the soil. The trowel can also be used to remove weeds and loosen compacted soil.

In addition, the trowel can be used to measure depth when planting and to make straight rows when sowing seeds.

Garden Spade

A garden spade is a tool to dig, plant, and transfer small amounts of materials like compost, soil, or mulch. It has a long, thin blade that is sharpened on one side and a D-shaped handle.

The blade is usually made of metal, and the handle is made of wood or plastic. Garden spades come in many sizes but have the same basic design.

Garden spades are used for various tasks, such as digging holes for planting, turning soil, transplanting seedlings or young plants, and moving small amounts of compost or mulch.

They can also be used to edge garden beds or to clean up leaves and debris. Garden spades are an essential tool for any gardener.

Garden Fork

Garden forks are one of the essential gardening tools. They come in various sizes and shapes, but they all have one common purpose: to loosen and aerate the soil.

Garden forks are used for multiple tasks, including turning compost, breaking up clumps of dirt, and aerating planting beds. They can also be used to weed vegetable gardens.

Garden forks have long, thin tines ideal for working in small spaces. The tines are also sharp enough to penetrate through challenging root systems.

Garden forks are typically made from steel or other durable materials, meaning they will last for years with proper care.

When choosing a garden fork, it is essential to consider the size of the tines and the width of the head.

Forks with shorter tines are better suited for turning compost and breaking up clumps of soil, while those with longer tines are better for aerating, planting and weeding flower beds.

Forks with wider heads are better for working in large spaces, while those with narrower heads are better for working in small areas. No matter what type of garden fork you choose, it will surely be a valuable addition to your gardening toolkit.

Garden Hoe

A garden hoe is a tool with a long handle and a flat blade. The blade is usually angled so it can easily move backwards and forwards through the soil. Garden hoes are used for various tasks, such as weeding, loosening up the soil, aerating, and making furrows for planting seeds.

Some hoes even come with a serrated edge, which can be used for cutting through tough roots or larger weeds. Whether a novice gardener or an experienced green thumb, a garden hoe is essential.

Garden Hose

The size of your garden area, the number of vegetable plants, and the type of water drainage your garden has will all affect the watering method you choose for your garden.

To water your plants, you can use a garden hose that has been leveled or held in your hand. When watering cans can't be used, hoses come in handy. A hose might be a better option if someone has physical limitations or cannot carry the weight of a filled watering can.

Watering Cans

A watering can is a container with a spout and handle designed for watering plants. Most watering cans are made from plastic or metal and have a large reservoir that can be filled with water. Some models also have a built-in sprinkler head, which makes it easy to distribute water evenly over a small area.

Watering cans are an essential tool for gardeners, as they provide a convenient way to deliver water directly to the roots of plants. A watering can is a crucial tool for maintaining the health and happiness of your vegetable plants, whether you are a veteran gardener or a novice.

Garden Gloves

Garden gloves are a type of glove that is specifically designed for use when gardening. They are usually made from a lightweight, breathable fabric that helps to keep your hands cool and comfortable while you work.

Garden gloves also have a textured grip that allows you to hold onto tools and planting materials. In addition, many garden gloves feature reinforced palms and fingers that help to protect your hands from thorns and sharp objects.

Whether you're an experienced gardener or just getting started, garden gloves can help you to get the job done while keeping your hands safe and comfortable. Since we'll be harvesting in the winter, we suggest using thermal gardening gloves.

Garden Wheelbarrow

A garden wheelbarrow is a small, practical vehicle designed to make light work of moving soil, plants and other gardening supplies around the yard. Wheelbarrows typically have a single wheel at the front and two supporting stands at the back, making them easy to manoeuvre even when fully loaded.

Many models also feature a tray or basket with low sides, making it easy to tip soil or plants without causing spillages. Garden wheelbarrows are an essential piece of equipment for any keen gardener.

They can be used for tasks such as moving soil from one part of the garden to another, transporting plants to and from the compost heap, or even ferrying tools and supplies between the shed and the plant beds.

Garden Trug

A garden trug is a small, shallow gardening container often used for harvesting fruits and vegetables. These trugs typically have handles on either side to make them easy to carry, and their shallow design makes them ideal for gathering herbs, greens, and other delicate plants.

Gardeners also use trugs for transporting soil, mulch, and other gardening supplies. While most trugs are made from wood or plastic, some artisans handcraft them from more unusual materials such as metal or bamboo. No matter what they are made from, garden trugs are an essential tool for any green thumb.

PREPARE YOUR SOIL: GARDEN SOIL 101

Your vegetable plants will need the right soil conditions to grow and thrive. Soil provides anchors for roots, stores water and nutrients, and moderates temperature changes.

The type of gardening soil you have will determine how well your plants will grow. For example, sandy soil drains quickly and doesn't retain nutrients well, while clay soil can be too dense for roots to penetrate. As a result, it's essential to understand the type of gardening soil you have so that you can provide the best possible conditions for your plants.

By identifying and understanding the importance of soil, you can ensure that your plants get the foundation they need to grow strong and healthy.

In addition to aiding in plant growth, the soil is crucial for providing plants with the nutrients we need when we eat them. Your harvest may not contain the essential nutrients you require if the ground you are planting your vegetables in is not healthy enough.

This means that you will be getting much less nutrition from them. Therefore, the soil impacts both your health and the vegetable plants.

FIVE TYPES OF SOIL

Silt Soil: This soil is a type of clay soil that is made up of tiny particles of organic matter, minerals, and rock. It has a high nutrient concentration, making it ideal for gardening.

However, silt soil can also be easily compacted, making it difficult for plants to grow. In addition, silt soil is susceptible to erosion, so it is vital to take care when watering plants. Despite these drawbacks, silt soil is still popular for gardening because it is easy to work with and provides good drainage.

Clay Soil: This is a type of soil that is made up of very fine particles; however, once bound together, they form lumpy, dense, and heavier soil. It is usually found near water sources, such as rivers and lakes. With this type of soil being relatively dense, it does not drain very well.

As a result, clay soil can be difficult to work with and challenging to grow plants in. However, there are some benefits to gardening in clay soil. One advantage is that clay soil is rich in nutrients, which can help plants to thrive.

Another benefit is that clay soil does not dry out as quickly as other types of soil, so that it can be helpful for drought-tolerant plants.

Sandy Soil: This is a type of light, airy soil that is composed of large particles of sand. It is also known as sandy loam or simply sand. Sandy soil is essential to many ecosystems and supports various plant life.

While sandy soil is often considered low in nutrients, it can be fertile if adequately managed. Sandy soil gardening requires a different approach than gardening in other types of soil.

For example, Sandy soil does not retain water well, so it is important to water plants more frequently.

Chalk Soil: This is a type of soil that is rich in calcium carbonate. It is typically found in areas with limestone bedrock, and it has a pH level that is higher than 7.

This type of soil is very alkaline, which can make it difficult for plants to take up nutrients. Also, chalk soil is very dense and compacted, making it difficult for roots to penetrate.

In addition, it is essential to note that chalk soil can dry easily so it is important to water plants regularly.

Loam Soil: This is a type of soil that is made up of clay, sand, and silt. This combination of particles gives loam soil its unique properties, which make it ideal for gardening. Loam soil can retain water and nutrients well while draining excess water quickly.

This makes it perfect for growing plants that require consistent moisture levels. In addition, loam soil is easy to work with and is not as prone to compaction as other types of soil.

However, loam soil can also be susceptible to drought and erosion if not correctly managed. Overall, loam soil is an excellent choice for gardening, provided that it is given the proper care and attention.

SIGNS OF HIGH-QUALITY AND FERTILE SOIL

You might have a few inquiries now that you know the value of healthy soil and the various soil types. You might wonder how you can tell if your soil is healthy or not, and what you can do to make it fertile enough to grow nutritious vegetables.

What Is Fertile Soil?

Fertile soil is rich in nutrients and can support different plant life. The ideal mix of fertility ingredients includes a balance of organic matter, minerals, gases, and water.

This unique combination provides the perfect environment for root growth while allowing water and air to reach plant roots. In addition, fertile soil is teeming with microbial activity, which helps to break down organic matter and release essential nutrients into the soil.

As a result, fertile soil is the key to a healthy and productive garden.

Fertile soil for vegetable gardening has the following characteristics:

- It has efficient internal water drainage.
- There's good moisture retention, although not drowning plants.
- It has essential minerals and nutrients.
- Its well-aerated soil allows air circulation and avoids the consequences of compaction.
- It's free of debris and pollution, such as stone and plastic.
- It's free from weeds and nutrient-stealing plants that prevent proper growth.
- It's free from infestations of worms or insects that pose a risk to the development of plants.
- It's rich in organic matter, such as compost or aged manure. Organic matter provides nutrients to plants. When a garden is rich in these resources, the soil will provide nutrients for the plants to grow, which means artificial fertilizers are often unnecessary.
- It doesn't feel compacted and hard.
- It's not too sandy, making the soil lose its nutrients.

STEPS TO PREPARE YOUR SOIL

Step 1: Test Your Soil

The quality of your garden soil has a significant impact on the health and vigor of your plants. By testing your garden soil, you can determine what nutrients it lacks and make adjustments to ensure that your plants get the nourishment they need to thrive.

Testing also allows you to monitor changes in your soil over time to identify any potential problems early on. There are a few different ways to test your garden soil. One standard method is to take a soil sample from several other garden areas and send it to a laboratory for analysis.

This will give you a detailed report of the nutrient content of your soil. Another option is to use a home testing kit, which will allow you to test for a limited number of nutrients— whichever method you choose; testing your garden soil is an integral part of ensuring a healthy and productive garden.

There are several different types of garden soil tests that you can perform to determine the quality of your soil. One popular test is the pH test, which measures the acidity or alkalinity of your soil. This is important because many plants have specific pH requirements to thrive.

Another standard test is the nutrient test, which measures the levels of essential nutrients like nitrogen, phosphorus, and potassium in your soil. This can help you determine whether or not your soil needs to be amended with fertilizer. Finally, the texture test allows you to determine the sand, silt, and clay proportion in your soil. This information can help you choose plants that will do well in your particular soil type. By performing these tests, you can get a better understanding of your soil and what it needs to produce healthy plants.

Step 2: Clean Your Soil

Many gardeners underestimate the importance of cleaning their garden soil. If you want to have a healthy garden, it is essential to get rid of all the debris and dirt that can accumulate over time.

Failing to do so can result in a build-up of harmful insects and diseases, quickly spreading to your plants and causing them to become sick.

In addition, contaminated soil can also lead to poor plant growth and a lackluster appearance. Luckily, cleaning your garden soil is relatively easy. Simply use a rake or hoe to remove any dead leaves or stems, and then use a shovel to turn over the top layer of soil.

This will help to aerate the soil and encourage new growth. With just a little effort, you can ensure that your garden soil is clean and healthy.

Step 3: Remove Infestations

Your garden is a haven for pests, diseases and weeds. These organisms can weaken your plants, reduce their yield, and make them more susceptible to stressors such as heat and cold. In some cases, an infestation can even kill your plants. Therefore, removing the infestation from your garden soil from the very beginning is essential.

If your garden soil is infested with pests, there are a few things you can do to get rid of them. One option is to solarize the soil, covering it with clear plastic for several weeks to trap it in the heat and eliminate pests.

Another option is to use Beneficial Nematodes, tiny creatures that eat the larvae of many common garden pests. You can also try using Insecticidal Soap, a safe and effective way to eliminate a wide variety of unwanted insects.

Whatever method you choose, getting rid of pests in your garden soil will help your plants to grow and thrive.

Step 4: Treat Your Soil

From the results of your soil laboratory testing or a home test kit, you can determine what your soil requires and lacks. It's crucial to follow up with your soil's needs once you understand its condition.

You can do a few simple things to treat and keep your garden soil healthy. First, add organic matter to your soil regularly. This can be in the form of compost, manure, or green waste; these all increase soil fertility. However, when using products, be sure to follow their instructions on when to use them, the quantity and how to apply them.

There's the option to purchase soil already fertile for your containers or raised beds in the scenario you've chosen not to plant in-ground. Utilizing this option means steps 1 to 3 is not required for container and raised bed gardens.

Second, avoid using chemicals, as they can damage the delicate balance of organisms in the soil. Third, aerate your soil regularly to encourage root growth and prevent compaction. By following these simple tips, you can keep your garden soil healthy and improve the chances of success for your vegetables.

STORE-BOUGHT VS HOMEMADE SOIL TREATMENTS

There are numerous ways to treat your soil; those methods can include using homemade or commercially produced products. You may prefer to buy products that are ready to use or get your hands dirty depending on the type of gardener you want; however, all options should be considered carefully as they each have their advantages and disadvantages.

HOMEMADE SOIL TREATMENTS

There are many benefits to creating your homemade soil treatments. By customizing the ingredients to your garden's needs, you can create a potent, effective concoction far superior to anything you could buy at the store.

In addition, homemade treatments are significantly cheaper than commercial products, and they allow you to avoid using harsh chemicals in your garden.

Perhaps most importantly, creating your soil treatments is an excellent way to get involved in the care of your plants and build a deeper connection to your garden.

Through trial and error, you will learn precisely what works best for your plants and develop a deep understanding of the delicate balance required for a healthy garden.

With a little effort, you can create a thriving, beautiful and nurturing garden.

Advantages

- You will save a lot of money and be able to make some treatments in bulk with already existing free ingredients.
- You will have a higher return on your investment.
- You can know the specific quantity of what you feed your vegetable crops, unlike store-bought treatments where you may speculate and hope you have enough of something.

Disadvantages

- The period it takes to make homemade treatments can be lengthy. It may be months before you finally use your compost and manure.
- You can't always be sure that your treatments give your vegetable plants precisely what they need. Extra testing for your homemade treatments may be necessary in some cases.
- It requires work on your part, such as constant maintenance and upkeep of the conditions of your treatments.

STORE-BOUGHT SOIL TREATMENTS

Every gardener knows that healthy soil is essential for growing strong plants. But what many don't realize is that store-bought soil treatments can be just as effective at achieving this goal if homemade soil treatment is not an option for you.

Not only do they provide essential nutrients, but they also help to improve drainage and prevent compaction. In addition, store-bought soil treatments can help reduce the time and effort required to maintain a healthy garden. They are an indispensable tool for any gardener who wants to save time and effort while getting the most out of their garden.

Advantages

- It saves you lots of time, as you buy products when you need them and use them when you need them.
- You don't have to wait months for treatment to mature before you use it.

Disadvantages

- It requires you to be mindful of the brands you pick and learn as much as you can about ingredients. This will help you avoid bad and potentially harmful soil treatments.
- Compared to homemade treatments, store-bought ones can be more costly when maintaining your garden.

DECIDING WHAT TO GROW

Before you head to the garden center to buy vegetables to plant, it is crucial to take some time to figure out which vegetables you would like to grow.

Not all vegetables are created equal, and each has unique requirements regarding soil type, sunlight, and water. For example, tomatoes require full sun and well-drained soil, while lettuce can tolerate partial shade and prefer damp soil.

By taking the time to choose suitable vegetables for your garden, you can set yourself up for success and ensure a bountiful harvest come harvest time.

Deciding what vegetables to grow in your garden can be a daunting task. There are countless options to choose from, and it can be challenging to know where to start. However, there are a few factors to consider before making your decision.

First, consider which vegetables you and your family enjoy eating; there is no point in growing vegetables that no one will eat.

Second, consider the climate in your area. Some vegetables require a warm environment, while others can tolerate cooler temperatures.

Third, think about the amount of space you have available. Some vegetables, such as tomatoes, need a lot of room to thrive, while others, such as herbs, can be grown in smaller pots. Considering all these factors, you can choose the best vegetables for your garden.

Additionally, it's important to remember that the soil in your garden can significantly impact what vegetable plants will thrive there. This is one of the main reasons why testing and understanding your soil is essential, as different plants have different nutrient requirements, so it is important to choose plants that can thrive in your particular soil.

Planting without fully understanding your soil conditions can cause your gardening efforts to be wasted, where you may feel disheartened and that you've failed when the problem is that the plant is in the wrong soil conditions.

Therefore, if you want a successful vegetable garden, you need to grow what will be the most successful for your soil type. As previously mentioned, techniques and products are available to alter your soil and achieve the desired requirements.

They are a surplus of ways to determine what vegetable is best for your garden. For example, if you want a vegetable supply that will last for months without replanting, you should grow vegetables that can regrow easily.

If you wish to do the least amount of work in your garden, grow vegetables that require little pruning and upkeep. If you want to save water in your garden, you should plant vegetables that require the least amount of water to grow strong.

You may also be deficient in a nutrient, such as vitamin A, and seek alternatives to vitamin supplements; you can then grow vitamin A-rich vegetables, such as broccoli and peas.

SOWING AND PLANTING SEEDS: SOW FAR, SOW GOOD

Now that you've decided what you want to grow, let's go over everything you need to know about getting started. Understanding how to plant and sow is vital for several reasons.

First, it can help you to choose the right location for your garden. Second, it can help you to select the appropriate plants for your area. Third, it can save you time and money by preventing problems such as overwatering or under watering.

Finally, it can also help you to enjoy your garden more by ensuring that your plants are healthy and vigorous. There are many different methods of planting and sowing, and each has advantages and disadvantages.

The key is to select the method that best suits your needs. For example, direct sowing is popular for many gardeners because it is quick and easy. However, it is essential to remember that this method can result in many weeds.

On the other hand, transplanting allows you to start with a smaller number of plants and then thin them out as they grow. This can be a more labor-intensive process, but it often results in fewer problems with weeds. No matter which method you choose, taking the time to understand the basics of planting and sowing will help you to create a beautiful and productive vegetable garden.

SOWING TECHNIQUES

Broadcasting

Broadcasting is a sowing method mainly for traditional outdoor gardens where seeds are scattered over the soil's surface.

This can be done by hand or using a mechanical broadcaster; once distributed, seeds may or may not be covered with soil.

Advantages

- It's one of the quickest methods.
- It's the cheapest method to sow seeds, especially for a large area when you don't have enough time or money to invest in other sowing methods.

- It can be used for container or raised bed gardens, as well.

Disadvantages

- It causes seed overcrowding.
- It's only suitable for seeds that don't need a specific amount of space to grow.
- It's only suitable for shallow-rooted plants.

Dribbling

The garden sowing method known as dribbling is a quick and easy way to sow small seeds. Simply take a small handful of seed, then cup your hand and let the seed fall through your fingers in a steady stream.

As you walk along, the seed will fall evenly across the ground. This method is particularly well suited for larger gardens, ensuring that the seed is distributed evenly. It also saves time, as there is no need to stop and start when sowing different garden sections.

However, dribbling is not suitable for all kinds of seeds. Smaller seeds, such as those used for salad greens, can be challenging to control with this method.

In addition, it is essential to be careful not to over-sow an area, as this can lead to overcrowding and poor plant growth. When used correctly, dribbling is an easy and efficient way to sow seeds in the garden.

Advantages

- It can be done in all types of gardens.
- It's a rapid and effective method.
- It's methodical and can be accurate if implemented correctly.

Disadvantages

- Can over-sow in areas, leading to overcrowding and poor plant growth.
- Not all vegetables can be sown using this method.

Plow Sowing

The garden sowing method, plow sowing, is a type of sowing method that is used for sowing crops in a field. This method is ideal for large areas, and it is also a very efficient method.

The plow sowing method involves using a tractor or cattle and a plow. The tractor or cattle is used to pull the plow through the field, and the plow is used for sowing the seeds.

This method can sow various crops, but it is most commonly used to sow wheat, barley, and oats. The plow-sowing method is a very efficient way to sow crops, and it is also very effective at preventing soil erosion.

Advantages

- It can be less costly when cattle are used.
- It's a fast way to sow seeds.
- It's great for large, traditional in-ground gardens.

Disadvantages

- It can be expensive, especially with plow machines.
- Seeds can become overcrowded.

Planting

The garden sowing method of planting is commonly used. This method entails making small depressions or holes in the ground with a tool, dropping seeds into the holes, and then covering them lightly with soil.

Once the seeds have been planted, they need to be watered regularly until they sprout and grow. The garden sowing method is a simple and effective way to plant your vegetables.

Advantages

- It allows you to be intentional in protecting fragile vegetable plants.
- It can be a quick process if you simply buy already germinated plants to grow.

Disadvantages

- It takes time before you can start planting if you are germinating the plants yourself.
- It can be costly if plants fail to grow time after time
- It's also time-consuming, as you would need to be very careful.

Transplanting

The garden sowing method of transplanting is a great way to start your plants. It involves taking seedlings that have already been grown in a controlled environment and moving them to your garden.

This ensures that the plants are already robust and have a head start on the growing season. Transplanting is also a great way to fill in gaps in your garden.

If you have a bare area, transplant some seedlings into the soil, and they will soon take root. With a bit of care, you can have a flourishing garden in no time.

Advantages

- It's a quick movement of plants.
- Transplanting makes it easy and possible to move plants across locations.
- You can rehabilitate plants and soil.

Disadvantages

- There's a chance of roots being damaged when done wrong.
- Not all plants may survive.
- A different soil may hurt or damage the plant when replanting.

READY, SET, GROW!

You've officially begun your exciting gardening journey now that you know how to sow your seeds! Wait and keep an eye on your garden.

Patience and consistency with the proper watering and maintenance schedule are both essential. It's critical to keep track of your garden's growth cycle and know exactly what to expect.

Each vegetable plant will grow differently, mature at a different rate, and so on. This growing season will reveal any problems with the soil, plants, or other issues that must be addressed. It's also an excellent time to use compost in your soil or other treatments to promote proper growth or to prevent bugs and further infestations that could ruin your garden.

Examine how the soil retains and drains the water, and remove any weeds, rocks and debris. If your vegetable plants are not getting enough sunlight and are suffering in their current location, you may need to relocate them.

This is simple if you have a container or raised bed garden; however, moving plants in a traditional in-ground garden may be difficult. This may necessitate replanting and moving plants to a better environment where they will receive adequate sunlight.

However if your planning stages were thorough prior to planting your seeds, you'll have nothing to worry about.

CHAPTER 2

GROWING YOUR WINTER ONIONS

A nyone who has ever cooked with onions knows that they can make even the simplest dish taste delicious. But did you know that onions are also incredibly nutritious?

They are a good source of fiber, vitamins A and C, and potassium. Plus, they contain antioxidants that can help boost your immune system. So why not grow your own onions? Not only will you get to enjoy their flavor, but you'll also know that they're fresh and healthy.

There are wide varieties of onions, and each has its flavor profile and culinary use. For example, red onions are best suited for raw dishes like salads, while sweet onions are ideal for cooked dishes like stews.

Regardless of your choice of variety, this chapter will walk you through the fundamentals and core practices of growing the freshest and ripest onions this winter.

THE RIGHT SOIL FOR ONIONS

To get these rich in flavor and savory onions as part of your winter harvest, you'll first need to understand the optimum soil conditions in which they thrive. Onions require nutrient-rich soil with good drainage.

Sandy loam or loamy sand soil is ideal where the soil should be loose enough so that the roots can spread easily. The onions will be small and lack flavor if the soil is too compacted. You'll also need to ensure the pH level is between 6.0 and 7.0.

Remember to use the various soil testing methods before purchasing treatments to avoid wasting your time, effort, and money. First, know exactly what your soil condition is, and then proceed with what exactly is needed for your soil.

You'll set yourself up for the best possible harvest with some research and preparation.

Onion Plant Diseases

Onions are a staple in many kitchens around the world. However, they are susceptible to several diseases that can cause damage to the bulbs and decrease yields. Here is a look at some of the most common onion diseases, as well as tips on how to spot and prevent them.

One of the most common onion diseases is downy mildew. This fungal disease thrives in cool, wet conditions and causes small, yellow spots to form on the leaves. If left unchecked, downy mildew can quickly spread to the bulbs, causing them to rot.

To prevent this disease, it is essential to water onions at the base of the plant rather than from above. This will help keep the leaves dry and reduce the chances of mildew spores.

Another common disease is white rot. This fungus affects the leaves and bulbs of onions, causing them to turn yellow and eventually decay. White rot is particularly damaging to onions because it can survive in even the driest conditions.

To control this disease, practicing crop rotation and avoiding planting onions in areas where the fungus has previously been present is essential. If you notice any signs of Onion plant diseases, it is crucial to take action immediately. Following these simple tips can help keep your onions healthy and productive for years to come.

Another cause of onion plant diseases can be by simply planting your crops in soil too close to certain vegetable types. Each vegetable requires different conditions; one will thrive while the other will not.

With a few notable exceptions, onions are generally friendly with everyone in the garden; however, onions should not be planted with:

- Beans (both pole beans and bush beans), peas, and other legumes
- Asparagus
- Sage
- Other plants in the onion family (garlic, leeks, shallots, chives, scallions) - Give them space because many diseases that attack one crop in the onion family can quickly transfer to a nearby crop in the same family.

In contrast, there are some vegetables that thrive and help onions thrive by planting them nearby. This practice is referred to as companion plantings which include the vegetables:

- Beets
- Broccoli, cabbage, cauliflower, kohlrabi, kale, and other brassicas.
- Lettuce.
- Peppers.
- Tomatoes.
- Carrots

For a final prevention method, it is critical to disinfect all tools used to touch infected plants and the soil, as failure to do so will spread the infection to other plants.

Use an alcohol disinfectant and hot water to clean the tools or equipment. Only after this process can they be used on other healthy plants.

HOW TO SOW ONIONS

Correct Season To Plant Onions

Onions are a versatile crop that can be harvested in spring and winter. However, as we plan to grow our harvest for winter, the correct time to plant is late summer or early fall. This ensures that the plants have enough time to mature and produce a good crop before the cold weather sets in.

Planting Needs And Requirements

For best results, onions should be transplanted into the garden rather than seeded directly into the ground. This will give them a head start on the growing season and allow them to mature more quickly. The process is relatively simple and only requires a few materials.

First, fill a seed tray with moistened organic matter or potting mix if you are unsure what matter to use (this will make sure you avoid any mistakes along the way with growing seedlings).

Then, place the onion seeds on the surface of the mix and lightly press them into the soil. Be sure to leave enough space between the seeds so that they have room to grow.

The number of seeds per container will depend on how large the plant container is. Cover the tray with a piece of plastic wrap or a lid and place it in a warm location.

Onion seeds will germinate at temperatures as low as 40 degrees Fahrenheit but most quickly at soil temperatures between 60 and 65 degrees Fahrenheit.

You don't need to germinate the onions seeds outside or in direct sunlight, as most seed germination is done indoors.

One of the reasons for this is to control the temperature the seeds are exposed to, ensuring they are warm enough, especially if you start germinating your seeds in spring and at the beginning of fall when it's starting to be a bit chilly outside.

Once the seedlings have emerged, they can withstand colder temperatures, down to 20 or 30 degrees Fahrenheit. However, if the temperature becomes too hot, onion seedlings will start to "bolt" or produce flowering stalks.

While onions that have bolted are still edible, they tend to be less flavorful than those that have been allowed to mature slowly. As a result, it is essential to monitor both the temperature and the size of your onion seedlings.

You can utilize a soil thermometer to ensure that the soil has the correct temperature. By taking regular readings of the soil temperature, you can ensure that your seedlings have the best chance of growing into strong and healthy plants.

Check on the seeds daily, adding water as needed to keep the mix moist; you can use a light spray to ensure that the seeds or seedlings are not drowning in water. In 10-14 days, the onion seeds should begin to sprout. At this point, you can remove the plastic wrap or lid and start watering the seedlings weekly in a sunny spot, also thinning out any crowded seedlings so that each one has room to grow.

Once they reach 6-8 inches tall, you can transplant them into individual pots or plant them outdoors in your garden. With a bit of patience and care, you can easily grow your onions from seed.

Spacing And Measurements

It's time to transplant your seedlings once you have them. You must ensure that the soil is moist but not soggy and has enough time to drain. You will take your seedlings out of their containers with the matter they have been growing in.

During this period, avoid damaging the seedlings or their roots because any harm may impede the onion plants' growth in the soil.

Planting onion seedlings is a simple process that can be completed in just a few steps. First, find an area of your garden that receives full sun and has well-drained soil.

Prepare the soil by raking it smoothly and removing any rocks or other debris. Then, loosen the soil to a depth of about six inches using a shovel or hoe. Next, create furrows in the loosened soil, spacing them about four inches apart. You can then carefully place the onion seedlings into the tracks, ensuring they are about four inches apart.

Finally, cover the seedlings with loose soil and water them lightly. Once the seedlings have been planted, keep an eye on them and water them regularly.

With a little care, your onion seedlings will soon be on their way to becoming fresh and ripe winter harvest.

WATERING ONIONS

You may want a specific guide on how much water is required when watering your onion plants; however, the frequency is determined by a couple of factors, such as temperature and the kind of soil you have.

As a gardener, you must be in tune with your garden and go through a phase of figuring it out. That means studying how well your soil absorbs water, how quickly, how long it stays moist, how your plants respond to your regular watering schedule, and how different temperatures affect your soil and your onion plants' watering needs.

All of this will help you determine a more solid and accurate idea as to how many times you should water it. However, there will be days when it rains, for example, and days like this will change your watering schedule; in the same way, other factors will also affect your watering schedule.

Always alter or adjust your watering schedule during the rainy season to prevent overwatering your onion plants. You can determine if your onions need more or less water by inspecting their soil, looking at it, and feeling it.

Sometimes, you might need to dig in the soil to check its moisture. It needs to be moist and not drenched or saturated in water.

How To Water Onions Plants

Onion plants need to be watered regularly, but unlike other vegetables, they have specific watering requirements. First, onion plants should only be watered in the morning hours. This allows the foliage to dry out before nightfall, which helps to prevent fungal growth.

Secondly, onions require a lot of water, so the soil should always be moist. To achieve this, it is best to water the plants deeply and less frequently rather than shallowly and more often.

This means watering deeply and thoroughly until the water has reached the bottom of the roots. To encourage deep rooting, consider using a soaker hose or drip irrigation.

These methods deliver water directly to the roots, with minimal evaporation or runoff. Finally, onion plants should never be allowed to sit in standing water. If the soil is too wet, the roots will start to rot, causing the plant to produce smaller bulbs.

You may also find mulch very useful in ensuring that your plants are protected from quick water evaporation and dryness in the soil. Mulch can be bought and poured on the surface of your soil and around your onion plants.

This also creates some insulation and keeps moisture in longer. By following these simple guidelines, you can ensure that your onion plants stay healthy and productive.

FERTILIZATION FOR ONIONS

Onions are a hardy crop that can be grown in various conditions, but to produce a strong and healthier crop, they need to be given the correct type of fertilizer at the right time.

The best time to fertilize onion plants is just before they start actively growing. For organic gardeners, compost or manure can be used instead of chemical fertilizers; manure is rich in nitrogen and other nutrients that onions need for healthy growth.

A balanced commercial fertilizer such as 10-10-10 or 11-11-11 can be applied at a rate of 1 pound per 100 square feet. It's important not to over-fertilize onions, as this can cause them to produce too much foliage and delay bulb formation.

If you're unsure how much fertilizer to use, it's better to err on the side of using too little rather than too much.

There are a few key things to keep in mind when fertilizing your onions; remember, you'll want to choose a fertilizer that is high in nitrogen.

This will help the leaves of your plant to grow green and lush. Secondly, you'll want to apply the fertilizer around the base of the plant, being careful not to get any on the leaves themselves. You'll also want to ensure that you water the fertilizer well into the soil so the roots can take up the nutrients.

By following these simple tips, you can give your onion plants the boost they need to grow strong and healthy.

How Often Do Onions Need Fertilization?

Onions are one of the most common and versatile vegetables in the world. They can be used in various dishes, and their intense flavor makes them a perfect addition to many recipes.

Given their popularity, it's no surprise that onions are a popular crop for farmers and home gardeners. But how often do onions need fertilization? The answer may surprise you.

Onions are heavy feeders, which means they require a lot of nutrients to grow properly. For this reason, onions should be fertilized on a regular basis.

A general rule of thumb is to apply fertilizer every four to six weeks during the growing season. However, some gardeners prefer to use fertilizer more frequently, especially young plants. It's essential to avoid over-fertilizing onions, as this can lead to leaf burn and other problems.

ONIONS GROWING STAGES

Before onions can make their way to your dinner table, they must first be grown. Depending on the type of onion, it can take anywhere from 70 to 120 days to mature. For example, onions grown in warm climates may develop faster than those grown in cooler temperatures.

Additionally, onions started from seed will take longer to mature than those started from transplants. While there is some variability, most onions will be ready to harvest within three to four months of planting.

PROTECTING YOUR ONIONS

Onion plants can be a target for onion flies and many other insects. It can be heartbreaking to one day walk up to your beautiful garden and discover that your onions have been attacked and eaten by something.

We're sure in that moment, your efforts may feel like they have been wasted; however, there are some ways you can protect your onion plants and prevent these heartbreaking possibilities and other threats.

Optimum Temperatures

Onions are a hardy vegetable that can withstand a wide range of temperatures, but there are a few temperature extremes that you should avoid if you want to produce a healthy crop. Firstly, onions cannot tolerate frost, so your plants will be damaged if the temperature drops below freezing. Secondly, onions prefer cool weather and will start to bolt (flower prematurely) if the temperature gets too hot. This will result in smaller and fewer flavor onions. For this reason, it's best to avoid planting onions in very hot weather.

Finally, onions need a period of vernalization (exposure to cold temperatures) to form bulbs. This means that you should avoid storing onions in warm conditions, as this will prevent them from bulbing up properly.

By considering the temperature when growing onions, you can ensure that you produce a healthy crop of flavorful bulbs.

Protect Onions From Pest

Onions are a favorite food for many insects, including aphids, thrips, and leek moths. These pests can quickly destroy an entire crop, making it essential for onion growers to take steps to protect their plants.

One way to deter insects is to grow onions in raised beds. This makes it more difficult for pests to reach the plants and allows for better drainage, which helps prevent rot.

In addition, onion growers can try using row covers or netting to create a physical barrier between the plants and potential pests. Regular applications of insecticidal soap or neem oil can help keep insect populations under control.

Keeping your garden clean and free of debris is vital, as this provides hiding places for pests. Another method is to try planting pest-resistant varieties of onions. These varieties have been bred to produce chemicals that deter pests.

Finally, make sure to harvest your onions as soon as they mature. Insects are more likely to attack overripe onions, so picking them early will help reduce the risk of infestation.

By taking these precautions, you can enjoy a bountiful harvest of healthy onions.

MAINTAINING YOUR ONION GARDEN

Pruning Onion Plants

Pruning onion plants is an integral part of their care. Doing this encourages the plant to put more energy into producing onions rather than foliage. It also helps to promote airflow, which can reduce the chances of fungal diseases developing.

Once your onions have reached about half their mature size, it's time to start pruning them. Start by removing any yellow or dead leaves. Use sharp shears to trim off the tops of the plants, leaving about 4 inches of growth. Make your cuts at a 45-degree angle, angling them away from the center of the plant.

This will encourage more side branching and prevent the center of the plant from getting too leggy. After pruning, water the plants well and apply a layer of mulch around them to help retain moisture. Continue to prune your onion plants every few weeks throughout the growing season.

When your onions plant may need structural support for growth, you can use a strong string or wire system to support your plants successfully. The string should be wrapped around the onion several times, with the ends secured to a nearby fence or trellis. This will give the onion the support it needs to grow tall and healthy.

HARVESTING ONIONS

One of the most rewarding experiences for a home gardener is harvesting their onion plants in winter. Onions are a cool-season crop, which means they can be planted in late summer/early fall. In most regions, onions are ready to harvest when the tops turn yellow and fall over. At this point, the bulbs will be about ¾ of their full size.

To harvest, lift the bulbs out of the ground with a gardening fork or trowel. Once they are out of the ground, brush off any excess dirt and let the onions cure in a warm, dry place for two weeks.

After they have cured, you can trim off the roots and tops and store the onions in a cool, dark place. You can enjoy fresh onions all winter long with a little care and patience!

SAVING ONIONS SEEDS

One way to ensure a plentiful supply of onions is to save the seeds from your best plants for replanting the following growing season.

First, let the onions ripen on the plant until the tops begin to brown and fall over. Cut off the onion tops, leaving about four inches of stem attached to the bulb.

Allow the onions to cure in a warm, dry place for two weeks. This helps to toughen up the skin and prevents rot. Once curing is complete, gently rub off the papery skin from the bulbs. Next, trim off the root end and any dried-out leaves.

Finally, cut off the onion top, then carefully peel away the outer layer of skin. You should now see the tiny, black seeds inside the onion. Gently remove them from the bulb and place them in a dry, well-ventilated container.

Store the container in a cool, dark place until you are ready to plant the seeds the following season. With a bit of care, your onions will provide an abundant crop for years to come.

CHAPTER 3
GROWING YOUR WINTER PEAS

Few things are more satisfying than eating a dish made with ingredients you've grown yourself. Peas are a relatively easy crop to grow, and they can be used in various ways - from soups and stews to salads and stir-fries. Peas are also a good source of vitamins and minerals, including vitamins C, K, and folate.

Pea plants are hardy and can withstand a light frost, making them a good choice for winter harvesting in many areas. Peas should be planted in late summer or early autumn for a winter harvest. This will give them enough time to develop before the weather becomes too cold. With a bit of care, you can enjoy fresh peas all winter long.

THE RIGHT SOIL FOR PEAS

To grow peas in winter, the soil must provide the plants with the necessary nutrients and moisture. The soil should be loose and well-aerated, allowing the roots to absorb water and nutrients easily. Peas also prefer slightly acidic soil, with a pH between 6.0 and 7.0. In terms of moisture, the soil should be kept evenly moist throughout the growing season.

Too much or too little water can lead to problems, such as poor plant growth or disease. The soil should be rich in organic matter, as this will help to improve its structure and drainage. Finally, it is crucial to test your soil before making any amendments.

The results from the test help select the right fertilizer and other amendments to add to the soil to improve plant growth; without this information, you may be wasting your time, money, and efforts.

Peas Plant Diseases

Pea plants are susceptible to several diseases, some of which can be deadly.

Some of the most common diseases that affect peas are powdery mildew, botrytis blight, fusarium wilt, and pea mosaic virus.

Powdery mildew is a fungus that affects the plant's leaves, causing them to become covered in a white powdery substance.

Botrytis blight is another type of fungus that affects the leaves and stems of the plant, causing them to rot.

Fusarium wilt is a soil-borne disease that affects the plant's roots, causing the leaves to turn yellow and wilt.

Pea mosaic virus is a virus that infects the leaves of the plant, causing them to become mottled or discolored.

Aphids and other insects spread the mosaic virus, and there is no known cure.

However, there are several ways to prevent these diseases from occurring. One way is to start with disease-free seeds or transplants. Another way is to practice crop rotation and avoid planting peas in the same spot.

Also, choose a well-drained site for planting peas and water them regularly. Finally, remove any infected plants from the garden as soon as possible to prevent the spread of the disease.

Unfortunately, once your plants have been infected, it's highly recommended not to replant in that same soil for some time.

It's also advised not to touch other plants or other pea plants with the same tools and equipment you have used for the infected ones. Prevent the spread of infection with an alcohol disinfectant and use hot water to wash your tools.

Plant diseases can also occur simply by planting certain types of vegetables too close to your pea crops, so with that in mind, it is best to practice avoiding planting peas next to vegetables such as:

- Onions
- Garlic
- Leeks
- Shallots
- Scallions
- Chives

HOW TO SOW PEAS

Correct Season To Plant Peas

The best time to plant peas for a winter harvest is in late summer or early fall when the weather is still warm, but the days are getting shorter. This allows the plants to establish themselves before the cooler temperatures set in.

Peas need a period of cool weather to produce their signature sweet flavor. If planted too late in the season, they will not have enough time to develop this flavor.

Peas need about 60 days to mature, so you want to ensure they have enough time to grow before the first frost. In most regions, that means planting them in August or September.

Peas are a cool-weather crop, so they actually prefer cooler temperatures and will even tolerate a light frost. However, if the temperature dips below freezing for more than a few days, the peas will damage and will not produce good yield.

So if you live in an area with unpredictable weather, it's best to err on the side of caution and plant your peas a little earlier in the season. You can enjoy a delicious winter harvest of fresh peas with proper care and attention.

Planting Needs And Requirements

The best way to germinate peas for winter harvest is by starting them indoors. You will need a pot or container at least 6 inches deep and fill it with a lightweight soil mix. Sow the pea seeds about 1 inch apart, and press them gently into the soil.

Water the seeds well, and then place the pot in a warm, sunny location. It's best to put one seed per pot, but you can put two in case the other dies or is not strong enough.

Keep the soil moist but not soggy; within 10-14 days, the seeds should begin germinating. Once they have sprouted, it is important to thin out the seedlings, so they are not over-crowded. Once the seedlings are large enough to handle, transplant them into individual pots or your garden bed.

To encourage pea plants to grow tall and produce abundant fruit, they must be provided with a support structure. One popular option is to build a simple trellis out of wood or metal. The trellis should be tall enough that the plants can reach the top, and it should be firmly anchored in the ground, so it does not tip over.

Another option is to plant the peas alongside a fence or other sturdy structure. If you do this, leave enough space between the plants, so they have room to climb. Whatever type of support you choose, monitor the plants regularly and remove any dead or damaged stems.

Spacing And Measurements

Once you have seedlings, you can then prepare to transplant them into the garden of your choice with a few simple steps. First, prepare the garden bed by loosening the soil and removing any stones or debris, and then create a shallow furrow in the soil using a garden hoe.

When planting peas, it is important to give them enough space to spread out, so it's recommended to plant peas two inches apart and in rows three feet apart. As previously mentioned, if you are growing a climbing variety of peas, you will need to provide some support for the vines to climb.

Next, carefully place the pea seedlings in the furrow and space them evenly. Finally, cover the seedlings with soil and water them gently. The pea plants will begin to sprout and grow within a few weeks.

MAINTAINING YOUR PEAS PLANTS

Although they require special care and upkeep, peas are not challenging to grow and maintain. You can grow them past the germination stage by following the steps listed.

Pruning Your Peas Plant

Peas are relatively easy to grow; however, they require some basic maintenance to produce a bountiful harvest. One of the essential tasks is pruning, which helps to encourage bushier growth and prevent the plants from becoming too leggy.

Pea plants should be pruned when they are about 12 inches tall. Using sharp shears, cut back the main stem to about 6 inches; this will encourage the plant to produce more lateral branches, creating more peas.

Remove any side shoots that are longer than 4 inches; once the plant has been pruned, it is essential to give it plenty of water and fertilizer to encourage new growth.

Watering Your Peas Plants

One of the most important things you can do for your pea plants is to water them properly. But how much water do they need, and how often should you water? The answer to these questions depends on several factors, including the type of pea plant, the stage of growth, and the weather.

In general, pea plants need about 1 inch of water per week. During hot, dry weather, you may need to water more frequently, as the plants will lose water more quickly through evaporation.

Once you are done watering your pea plant, you can pour mulch on the surface of the soil; this is, so the moisture and warmth remain in the soil for as long as possible, as well as to prevent pests.

Only water your pea when the soil needs more; otherwise, avoid watering. You can tell if your plants need watering if the leaves start to wilt or the stems droop.

To water your plants, use a soaker hose or drip irrigation system to apply water slowly to the base of the plant. Be careful not to overwater, as this can drown the roots and promote fungal growth. With a little care and attention, you can ensure that your pea plants get the water they need to thrive.

Fertilization For Peas

Nitrogen, phosphorus, and potassium are essential nutrients for pea plants, and each plays a different role in plant growth. Nitrogen is responsible for leaf and stem growth, phosphorus helps to promote root growth, and potassium aids in the development of flowers and fruits.

A lack of one of these nutrients can result in stunted growth or poor yields. Pea plants are susceptible to nitrogen levels, so it is essential to use a fertilizer that contains a good balance of all three nutrients.

When grown in soil, peas typically need little to no fertilizer. A small amount of fertilizer, such as 5-10-10, may be applied early in their growth if grown in a container.

Many different types of fertilizer are available, but organic options are often best for pea plants. Composted manure or blood meal are excellent choices for providing pea plants nutrients; adding some organic matter to the soil before planting can also help to improve yield and plant health.

PROTECTING YOUR PEAS

Extreme Temperatures

Pea plants are relatively resilient and can tolerate a wide range of temperatures, but there are a few extremes that they cannot survive. If the temperature drops below freezing with levels as low as 28 Degrees Fahrenheit, the water inside the plant cells will expand and cause the cell walls to burst.

This damage is irreversible, and the plant will die. Similarly, if the temperature gets too hot, reaching a level of 85 Degrees Fahrenheit, the plant cells will begin to break down due to dehydration. Once again, this damage is fatal.

As a result, pea plants should be protected from extreme cold and heat to ensure their survival. Your pea plant will flourish by planting within the advised seasons and months.

Protect Peas From Pests

As any gardener knows, pests can be a severe problem for plants. Left unchecked, they can quickly destroy a crop, causing extensive damage and financial losses. Peas are particularly vulnerable to pests due to their delicate nature.

Several pests can damage pea plants, including aphids, weevils, and nematodes. To protect your plants, it is essential to identify the signs of an infestation and take steps to prevent the pests from harming your crops.

Aphids are small, winged insects that feed on the sap of plants. They are often found in clusters on the undersides of leaves. Aphids can cause stunted growth and distorted leaves. To control aphids, use an insecticidal soap or spray.

Weevils are small beetles that feed on the leaves of pea plants. The larvae live in the soil, and emerging adults can cause extensive damage to crops. To prevent weevil damage, plant resistant varieties of peas and practice crop rotation.

Nematodes are tiny worms that live in the soil and feed on plant roots. Nematode infestations can lead to stunted growth, yellowing leaves, and wilting. To control nematodes, solarize the soil or use a nematicide.

You can also use some general practices and tips to protect your pea plants from pests. First, keep your garden clean and free of debris. This will remove potential hiding places for pests and make it easier to spot them if they do appear.

Next, regularly check your plants for signs of pest damage. Look for things like holes in leaves, chewed stems, or webbing. If you spot any of these signs, take action immediately to isolate the affected plant and prevent the spread of the infestation.

Consider using natural pest control methods such as companion planting or traps. These can be effective at deterring pests without resorting to harmful chemicals. Following these tips can help keep your pea plants healthy and free from pests.

HARVESTING PEAS

The process of harvesting peas is relatively simple and only requires a few tools. Peas are ready to harvest about 60-70 days after planting. This is excellent news if peas are one of your favorite vegetables because you won't need to wait too long for harvest compared to other vegetable plants.

As peas mature, the pods will swell and begin to turn yellow. To check if your peas are ready to harvest, open up a pod and see if the peas inside are plump and green.

If so, it's time to start harvesting; if they are not quite ready, you can leave them on the vine for a few more days. You can also test by gently squeezing a few pods. If they're ready, the peas will be visible and easy to push out of the pod.

Peas can be harvested by hand or with a mechanical harvester. If you are harvesting by hand, use your fingers or pruning shears to cut the stem above where the pea pod attaches.

Check all peas in a pod before picking, as some may be ripe while others are not. Look for plump and green pods, and avoid any that are yellow or brown. Once you have collected a good amount of peas, open up the pods and remove the peas.

Once you have harvested your peas, you can either eat them fresh or store them for later use. Place peas in a perforated bag and put them in the refrigerator or freezer to store them. Peas will stay fresh for about a week in the fridge or for six months in the freezer.

SAVING PEA SEEDS

Pea plants are annuals that produce delicious and nutritious peas. Each pea pod contains several seeds, and pea plants often produce more pods than a gardener can eat. As a result, many gardeners choose to save pea seeds so they can plant them the following year.

To do this, wait until the peas are fully mature, dried, and turned brown on the vine. Then, cut off the pod and open it to remove the seeds. Next, spread the seeds on a paper towel and let them air dry for a few days.

Once they are dry, store them in an airtight container in a cool, dark place. Pea seeds will remain viable for several years if stored properly.

Saving your pea seeds is a great way to reduce your gardening costs and ensure that you have a steady supply of plants. It is also a fun way to create your unique varieties of peas. Try mixing different peas to see what interesting new colors and flavors you can create.

CHAPTER 4

GROWING YOUR WINTER BRUSSELS SPROUTS

Some people might turn their nose up at the thought of growing their own Brussels sprouts, but there are many benefits to this hardy little vegetable.

First, Brussels sprouts are relatively easy to grow and are reasonably low maintenance. They can be planted in early spring and will continue to produce sprouts until early winter. In addition, Brussels sprouts are a great source of nutrients, including vitamins C and K.

They are also high in fiber and antioxidants. Not to mention, growing your Brussels sprouts can save you money in the long run. So whether you are a seasoned gardener or a beginner, if you're looking for a healthy and affordable vegetable to add to your garden, consider growing Brussels sprouts and enjoy fresh, delicious, and healthy veggies all season long.

THE RIGHT SOIL FOR BRUSSELS SPROUTS

Brussels sprouts love the cooler weather of fall and winter and will produce sweeter sprouts if exposed to a few frosty nights before harvest. With a little planning and care, it is possible to enjoy a bountiful harvest of these tasty little cabbages well into the colder months.

The key to success is in choosing the right soil conditions. Brussels sprouts thrive in rich, loamy soil high in organic matter that can retain moisture but not become waterlogged, preventing root rotting and other plant diseases.

They also prefer soils with a slightly acidic pH in the range of 6.0 to 6.8. So if your soil is too alkaline, you can lower the pH by adding sulfur or peat moss. However, test your soil before making any alterations or amendments.

We may sound like a broken record repeating this over and over, but we say this to stress the importance of this stage during your gardening journey.

Brussels Sprouts Plant Diseases

Brussels sprouts must be continuously inspected like any other vegetable plant for diseases, viruses, bacteria, and fungi that could harm or kill them.

Nothing is more upsetting than having everything in place, finally putting your seedlings in their permanent soil, and then having your plants die a few weeks later. While discouraging, this is easily preventable with proper diligence and effort.

Some of the most common diseases include Alternaria leaf spot, black rot, bottom rot, clubroot disease, and downy mildew. To detect these diseases, keep an eye out for brown or yellow spots on the leaves, stunted growth, wilting or dying leaves, and white or gray mold on the undersides of the leaves.

If you notice any of these symptoms, you must take action immediately.

Fortunately, a few measures can be taken to lessen the impact of diseases on plants. One step is to choose disease-resistant varieties whenever possible.

For example, many Brussels sprouts are now bred to resist common diseases like leaf spots and downy mildew. Another approach is to practice preventive care, such as keeping weeds under control and providing adequate ventilation for plants.

It is essential to regularly inspect your plants for signs of disease; early diagnosis is key to preventing severe damage. If you see any unusual spots or coloration on the leaves, remove the affected leaves immediately and dispose of them in the trash.

Destroy any diseased plants as well, as they can quickly spread disease throughout your garden. It is essential to avoid overhead watering and to water at the base of the plant; this will help prevent water from splashing onto the leaves and spreading disease.

Finally, when planting your Brussels sprouts, it is best practice to avoid planting in the same soil as a few vegetables.

These vegetables are known to take away nutrients from your plants; as a result, your plants are weakened and highly susceptible to the previously mentioned diseases. The following vegetables are:

- Potatoes
- Eggplants
- Mustard Greens
- Peppers
- Tomatoes

Following these simple guidelines can help ensure a healthy harvest of Brussels sprouts.

HOW TO SOW BRUSSELS SPROUTS

Correct Season To Plant Brussels Sprouts

Fall is the perfect time to plant Brussels sprouts for a winter harvest. These hardy vegetables are well-suited to cold weather and can provide a delicious winter harvest. Planting in the fall gives the plants time to develop strong roots before the weather turns cold.

The roots will anchor the plant and help it to withstand heavy rains and high winds. When choosing a planting site, select an area with full sun and well-drained soil.

Although Brussels sprouts can tolerate some light shade, they will produce the best yield when grown in full sun. Once the plants are established, they can withstand temperatures as low as 20 degrees Fahrenheit.

Planting Needs And Requirements

One of the best ways to ensure a bountiful harvest of Brussels sprouts is to start the plants from seeds indoors. Germinating Brussels sprout seeds is a simple process that requires patience.

First, fill a planting tray with seed-starting mix and water it until it is evenly moist. Then, sow two to three seeds about half inch apart and half inch deep. It's always advised to put more than one seedling in each container to offset any possible loss. That way, you don't lose out on your time if a seedling fails; instead, you will replant the other seedling that has already germinated from the same container.

Cover the tray with plastic wrap or a lid to create a humid environment that will encourage germination. Place the tray in a warm location from direct sunlight, and check on it daily to ensure the soil stays moist; however, ensure not to oversaturate them. After about 7 - 10 days, the seeds should begin to sprout. Since you would have planted more than one seed in each container, you need to watch for the best-growing seedlings in each.

Once they have reached about 2 inches tall, you can transplant the seedling into a larger pot or directly into your garden beds. At all times, make sure conditions are between 68-86 degrees Fahrenheit for optimum growth.

Prime germination usually occurs between 77-83 degrees Fahrenheit. If the temperature is too low, it will take longer for the seeds to germinate. If the temperature is too high, the seeds may not germinate.

Spacing And Measurements

Typically, Brussels sprout plants must be planted in the ground rather than in pots or raised bed gardens. Neverthe-less, it is possible to grow Brussels sprouts in a container or raised bed; you might be limited in how many you can grow, but it is possible.

First, choose a sunny spot, be sure that this spot will have full sun exposure, as Brussels sprouts need at least six hours a day of sun exposure.

Once you have selected the location, dig a hole twice as wide and deep as the current pot. Gently loosen the soil around the roots of the plant, and gently lift the seedlings out of the pots, being careful not to damage the roots.

Place the plant in the hole of the new pots or beds, ensure the roots are well-covered, and firmly press the soil around the plant. Once planted, be sure to water your plant, ensuring the soil is moist; however, be careful not to overdo it, as this can lead to root rot.

When growing Brussels sprouts, it is important to space the plants properly to ensure proper growth and development. The plants should be spaced approximately 18 inches apart, with 36 inches between rows.

Some varieties of Brussels sprouts may not need that much space, as they all vary in size. However, 18 inches apart should accommodate all.

MAINTAINING YOUR BRUSSELS SPROUTS

Brussels sprouts can be pretty simple when you know what to do and how to do it. Brussels Sprouts plants are not overly demanding or troublesome if adequately cared for. We'll go over some of the simple but effective ways your Brussels Sprouts plants require care and love to thrive.

Pruning Your Brussels Sprouts

Pruning your Brussels sprouts is integral to keeping them healthy and productive.

Make sure that you are always looking out for any yellow or dying leaves; cut them off the plant and any suckers that are growing from the base of the plant. By doing so, you give the plant more energy to put towards creating new ones.

For best results, cut the main stalk back to about one-third. This will encourage new growth, preventing the plant from becoming leggy and encouraging the plant to produce more side shoots, which will result in more sprouts.

In some cases, you may have spaced your Brussels sprouts too close to each other, or they may have overgrown and are tightly locked. You will then need to remove some Brussels sprouts to create the necessary space for proper growth.

This process is often referred to as "thinning." It may seem counterproductive, but it can be necessary, especially when the overcrowding causes your Brussels sprouts not to grow correctly, attract infestations and other issues.

Generally, pruning helps to keep the plant's size under control. Left unchecked, a Brussels sprout plant can quickly become overgrown and difficult to manage, causing various unwanted issues.

Regularly pruning the plant can ensure that it stays healthy and manageable. With proper care and pruning, you are one step close to producing fresh and ripe Brussels sprouts for your winter harvest.

Watering Brussels Sprouts

Winter is the time of year when plants go dormant, and many gardeners assume that this means they don't need to water their crops. However, this is not the case for Brussels sprouts.

Brussels sprouts are heavy feeders, and to produce a winter harvest, these hearty vegetables need to be watered regularly throughout the fall. These vegetables are sensitive to both too much and too little water.

Too much water can lead to fungal diseases, while too little water will cause the sprouts to become small and rugged. The best way to water Brussels sprouts is to give them a deep watering once a week.

This means watering the soil around the plants rather than just spraying the leaves, this will ensure that the plant gets all the water it needs, and it will help you avoid any infections or diseases.

Always consider the weather; if it has been raining, you may need to skip watering for a week, depending on how the soil feels and looks. The first three inches of soil should be moist; if they aren't, it's a sign that you need to water it more.

Mulching the soil around the plants can also help to preserve moisture levels. Organic mulch, such as straw or chopped leaves, will also help to keep weeds at bay.

When watering, be sure to avoid wetting the leaves of the plants too much, as this can promote fungal growth. Water early in the day so the leaves have time to dry before nightfall.

With some care, you can ensure that your Brussels sprouts get just the right amount of water and stay healthy all season long.

Fertilization For Brussels Sprouts

Fertilization is an essential part of growing healthy Brussels sprouts. The right mix of nutrients will help the plants to thrive and produce plenty of tasty sprouts. There are a few things to consider when fertilizing Brussels sprouts.

First, plants need a good amount of nitrogen for solid growth. A second essential nutrient is phosphorus, which helps plants to produce more flowers and fruits.

Finally, potash (potassium) is necessary for ensuring that the plants don't become stressed by extreme weather or pests.

A well-balanced fertilizer will provide all of these nutrients in the right proportions, so it's advised to use a time-based granular fertilizer with an NPK of 10-10-10 or 5-10-5, or 5-10-10. It's worth noting that the best time to fertilize is in the fall before the plants begin to produce buds.

Water the fertilizer into the soil to help it reach the roots of the plants. Remember that too much fertilizer can damage the plants, so it is essential to follow the instructions on the package carefully.

PROTECTING YOUR BRUSSELS SPROUTS

Unfortunately, Brussels Sprouts can be delicate and are often susceptible to damage from pests or inclement weather. Fortunately, there are a few simple steps that you can take to protect your Brussels sprouts and ensure a bountiful harvest.

Extreme Temperatures

When growing Brussels sprouts, it is important to be aware of the potential of extreme temperatures. Hot weather above 80 degrees Fahrenheit can cause the plants to bolt, resulting in tiny, bitter-tasting sprouts.

On the other hand, extreme cold weather with levels as low as 20 degrees Fahrenheit can damage the leaves, making them more susceptible to pests and diseases; as a result, it is essential to monitor the temperature closely when growing Brussels sprouts.

Pay attention to both the air temperature and the soil temperature. If either gets too high or too low, take steps to protect the plants. For example, you may need to provide extra water or shade during hot weather or apply a layer of mulch during cold weather; additionally, you can also use frost cloth, but make sure that it is loose enough to allow air to circulate.

It is also essential to choose a variety of Brussels sprout suited to your climate. Some types are more heat-resistant than others, so if you live in a warm climate, it's worth selecting one of these varieties. Taking precautions against extreme temperatures can help ensure that your Brussels sprouts are healthy and delicious.

Protect Brussels Sprouts From Pests

Brussels sprouts are a popular vegetable often used in salads, soups, and stir-fries. The small, green heads of the plant are packed with nutrients and have a slightly bitter taste.

Unfortunately, Brussels sprouts are also a favorite food of many pests, including root maggots, caterpillars, and aphids which not only eat your cabbage plants but lay eggs on them —setting you back big time.

However, using collars around the base of your Brussels sprout can significantly reduce the risks of maggots or worms reaching your plants. It may seem simple and ineffective, but it does help a lot, and it's worth trying.

There is no need to buy special plant collars for your plant because you can use some cardboard or any type of material that won't harm your plants. You can cut them out in circles; make a straight cut to the hole in the middle to open up and put it around the bottom stem of your plants.

To secure the collar, staple the slit to ensure it won't move or let the pests through. One of the ways to prevent the maggots is to put the collar around the stem onto the soil bed soon after planting them so you don't give the maggots time to lay eggs around the plant.

You can also plant dill or mint around your plant to protect them from mites or aphids. Thyme can also be planted next to your Brussels Sprouts garden to protect them from worms. That's because thyme acts as a repellent against worms.

All these types of plants serve not only as repellents but are used as sacrificial plants in some cases, where the pest will rather eat and destroy them instead of the plant.

Finally, make sure to keep the area around the plants free of weeds and debris, as they can attract pests and provide a place to hide. If you notice any pests on the plants, you can remove them by hand or use an organic insecticide soap, which will get rid of the unwanted pests and preserve the helpful ones. By taking these simple steps, you can help to keep your Brussels sprouts safe from harm.

HARVESTING BRUSSELS SPROUTS

Once planted, Brussels sprouts usually mature between 80 to 105 days. The time can vary depending on the type of variety you are planting, the season you are planting in, fertilization and more.

However, you will know your Brussels sprouts are ready to be harvested when the heads are firm, the leaves are green, and the sprouts are about an inch in diameter.

If you harvest the sprouts too early, they will be tough and bitter, so it's best to wait for the specific harvesting time, as Brussels sprouts also become sweeter after a few light touches of frost.

If you wait too long, the sprouts will begin to fall off the plant and will be past their prime. To ensure that your sprouts are of the best quality, check them regularly and pick them up as soon as they are ready.

Harvesting Brussels sprouts is a simple process that can be done with just a few tools. First, equip yourself with a sharp pruning tool and a large bowl.

Look for healthy stalks that are at least 18 inches tall. Cut the stalk about two inches below the sprouts, careful not to damage the roots. As you cut each stalk, place it in the bowl. Once you have collected all of the Brussels sprouts, bring them inside and wash them thoroughly.

Finally, trim any yellow leaves and enjoy your delicious, home-grown harvest.

Sprouts may be stored in one of three ways after harvest. A method is to leave them on the stem and hang them in a cool, dark place—ideally, a shed with appropriate protection.

They can last up to a month if done in this manner. You could also remove the sprouts from the stem and store them in your refrigerator.

They will last roughly a week. To Freeze them, remove any dead or discolored leaves and blanch them in boiling water for a few minutes, then immediately submerge them in cool water. They will last about six months once stored in freezer bags directly after.

SAVING BRUSSELS SPROUT SEEDS

The process of saving Brussels sprout seeds is not complicated, but it requires patience. First, allow the sprouts to mature on the stalk until they are dry and brown. For 1-2 weeks, it is recommended to leave the harvested stalks to cure.

To harvest the seeds, rub the dried heads between your hands to release them. Once released, seeds should be left to dry in partial sun. Store your dried seeds safely in an airtight container, where your seeds can last for at least three years.

CHAPTER 5

GROWING YOUR WINTER HERBS (ROSEMARY, OREGANO & THYME)

Winter can be a difficult time for gardeners. With the cold weather and shorter days, it can be tough to keep plants alive, let alone thrive; especially when discussing delicate herbs.

However, several winter herbs can be grown indoors, providing flavor and decoration for your home. Rosemary, thyme, and oregano are all herbs that do well in colder weather and can provide a welcome splash of green during the dark winter months.

In addition to their visual appeal, these herbs can add flavor to your cooking. Rosemary is a versatile herb that pairs well with meats and vegetables, while thyme is a common ingredient in soups and stews. Oregano can also be used in various dishes, from pizza to pasta sauce.

On top of this, growing herbs indoors can help purify the air in your home and provide a much-needed dose of green during the winter months. So if you're looking for a way to brighten up your home during the winter months, consider growing some winter herbs indoors.

THE RIGHT SOIL FOR HERBS

Growing herbs indoors is an excellent option for anyone looking to add a touch of flavor to their home-cooked meals. Rosemary, thyme, and oregano are all fairly straightforward to grow and can be easily incorporated into various recipes. However, choosing the right type of soil for these herbs to thrive is essential.

The best soil for these plants is a well-draining, sandy loam with pH levels of 5.0 - 7.5. This type of soil has a high percentage of organic matter, which helps to hold moisture and nutrients. Additionally, sandy loam soil drains well, preventing the roots from becoming waterlogged.

To ensure adequate drainage, add perlite or vermiculite to the potting mix. These amendments help improve aeration and drainage while keeping the soil light and loose.

Although most herbs can grow within the soil conditions of 5.0 - 7.5 pH levels, each plant has its optimum conditions, ensuring the best yields are produced. For example, oregano will grow best between 5.8 – 6.2 pH levels, rosemary between 5.0-6.0, and thyme between 5.5 – 7.0.

If you want to have a successful yield of herbs for your winter harvest, it is vital to know the condition of your soil. This is especially true since we'll be growing our plants indoors and in containers.

Unlike grown in the ground, container-grown plants rely on you to provide them with all the nutrients they need. As a result, it is essential to test your soil regularly and make adjustments as needed.

For a refresher, you can head back to our first chapter, where we covered the different ways to test your soil. Remember, by taking the time to test your soil; you can be sure that your plants are getting the nutrients they need to thrive.

Winter Herbs Plant Diseases

Winter is a tough time for herb plants. The cold weather and lack of sunlight can make them susceptible to diseases damaging the leaves, stems, and roots.

Some common winter herb diseases include powdery mildew, rust, and leaf spot.

Powdery mildew is a fungal disease that forms a white powder on the plant's leaves.

Rust is another fungal disease that appears as orange or red spots on the leaves.

Leaf spot is caused by bacteria or fungi and appears as small brown or black spots on the leaves. These diseases can weaken the plant and make it more susceptible to other problems.

However, as we'll be growing our herbs indoors, the likely hood of the mentioned diseases occurring is almost non-existent. How and why, you may ask? This is because growing herbs indoors is a great way to prevent plant diseases from taking hold.

By controlling the environment, you can create the perfect conditions for your plants to thrive. When grown indoors, herbs are less likely to be exposed to wind and extreme temperatures that can cause plants to become stressed.

Growing herbs indoors will allow you to control the amount of water your plants receive. Overwatering is one of the most common ways that plants become diseased.

Due to the natural fortification and protection of growing plants indoors, the pest that can spread diseases from plant to plant is less likely to be a problem as they do not have the means to access and infect your plants. As a result, they are better able to resist disease and remain healthy.

Additionally, growing herbs indoors will allow you to monitor your plants closely and catch any problems early on. It's essentially a win-win growing your herbs indoors. So with some care, you can enjoy a bountiful harvest of healthy herbs this winter.

HOW TO SOW HERBS

Correct Season To Plant Herbs

When it comes to growing your herbs indoors, the question that should be asked is, "what is the ideal growing conditions" rather than "what is the correct season to plant your herbs." This is because our conditions and environment will dictate how well our plants thrive, so it is crucial to understand what conditions is best for our plants before we start cultivating.

For many herbs, the ideal growing conditions are bright sunlight with at least six hours of direct sunlight per day and well-drained soil.

These conditions are relatively easy to recreate indoors with the following guidance. A south-facing window is the best option for achieving bright sunlight because it faces the direction in which the sun is located in the sky.

This allows the sunlight to enter the room more directly, resulting in a brighter and more consistent light. Alternatively, the use of grow lights can be used to achieve the same objective.

To create soil with great drainage, plant your herbs in pots with drainage holes and use a well-draining potting mix.

Once you've created the optimum environment, you can be sure that you've given your herbs plant the best chance to grow into the fragrant and flavorful addition to your harvest.

Planting Needs And Requirements

One of the best things about herbs is that they are relatively easy to grow, even for novice gardeners. Germinating herb seeds indoors is a relatively simple process that allows you to control the growing environment.

As we previously mentioned, most herbs need full sunlight in order to flourish, so it is vital to choose a spot near a window where they will receive plenty of light.

Once you have selected a location, you will need to fill your pots or seed trays with potting mix or seed-starting mix and lightly water the soil. Once watered, simply scatter the seeds on the soil's surface and lightly press them down.

Finally, place a sheet of glass or plastic over the top of the tray or pot to create a mini greenhouse effect. Keep the soil moist but not soggy; you should see little green sprouts poking through the soil within a few weeks.

For each herb, the germination process may vary slightly in time, so here are some guidelines to follow during this process.

Rosemary: The germination period for rosemary seeds is usually between 10 -14 days at temperatures between 65 – 85 degrees Fahrenheit.

Thyme: The germination period for thyme seeds is usually between 21-28 days at temperatures of 70 degrees Fahrenheit.

Oregano: The germination period for oregano seeds is usually between 8 -14 days at temperatures of 70 degrees Fahrenheit.

Spacing And Measurements

Now that your seeds have germinated into seedlings, it is time to transplant them into their new and permanent location. As we'll be growing our herbs indoors, our choice of growing medium will be containers.

When choosing containers for your plants, there are three main factors to consider: the size of the container, the material it is made of, and whether or not it has suitable drainage holes.

The first thing to think about is the size of the container. Herbs generally don't need much space, so a small pot or window box should be sufficient.

However, if you intend to grow a larger indoor garden, you may need multiple pots, bigger pots, or even entire shelves dedicated to your plants.

Not only is it essential to select a container that can house your chosen amount of plants, but it is also deep enough for the plant's mature root structure.

It's advised to always err on the side of caution and select containers that are a little bit larger than what the plants may require.

Next, consider the material of the container. There are three preferred and popular choices when selecting containers for growing herbs indoors.

These are terra cotta, plastic, or fiberglass containers. Pots made of plastic or fiberglasses are portable and available in various dimensions, colors, and shapes.

They are affordable, which is great for reducing out-of-pocket costs. Although they are heavy and breakable, terra cotta pots are solid and long-lasting.

Additionally in order to prevent the soil from becoming waterlogged, air movement through the pots and growing medium is great at controlling soil moisture levels. This is why choosing the correct type of pot is essentials.

Finally, you'll want to ensure that the container has drainage holes to allow excess water to escape. Overwatering is a serious issue because it reduces soil oxygen levels and damages your plants' root systems.

Now that we've successfully selected our containers for growing, it's time to create and fill them with the optimum soil conditions to grow our seedlings.

As previously mentioned, oregano will grow best in conditions of 5.8 – 6.2 pH levels, rosemary between 5.0-6.0, and thyme between 5.5 – 7.0 pH levels. Be sure to check that your soil meets these requirements before planting.

Now it's time to gently remove the seedlings from their current pots or trays; loosen up any bound roots, then plant the seedlings in the soil, ensuring they are at the same depth they were in their previous home.

Gently pat down the soil around them, then water it until it is moist but not soggy, finally placing your containers in a sunny location.

As each herb plant varies in size, it's essential to know and plant your herbs with enough space to allow them to grow to their matured heights. So here are some guidelines which can be used when planting your seedlings.

Rosemary seedlings should be planted 1 – 3 inches apart, oregano seedlings should be planted 8 – 12 inches apart, and thyme seedlings should be planted 9 inches apart. With the provided guidance's a little care and love, your herb seedlings will soon be ready to harvest.

MAINTAINING YOUR WINTER HERBS

Pruning And Thinning Your Winter Herbs

Like most people, you probably think of pruning as something you only do to outdoor plants. However, pruning is also an essential part of caring for indoor herbs.

Most indoor herbs need to be pruned to stay healthy and produce the best possible flavor; waiting until the plant is actively growing before pruning is best.

As a general rule of thumb, herbs that flower should be pruned after they bloom, while those that do not flower can be pruned at any time.

When it comes to pruning herbs, less is usually more. Removing just a few leaves or stems at a time is better than taking off too much at once.

This will help control the size and shape of your plants and allow them to recover quickly, preventing them from becoming stunted or leggy.

While the general principles of pruning are the same for indoor and outdoor plants, there are a few things to remember when pruning your indoor herbs.

First, ensure that you have a sharp pair of shears or scissors. This will help to prevent damage to the plant. Second, try to prune in the morning or evening when the temperature is cooler. This will minimize stress on the plant.

Finally, don't be afraid to experiment. Every plant is different, so you may need to try different techniques to find what works best for your herbs. With a bit of practice, you'll be an expert at pruning your indoor herbs in no time.

Watering Your Winter Herbs

If you're lucky enough to have a windowsill garden or just a few potted herbs on the kitchen counter, you'll need to give them regular watering.

But how often and how much water do indoor herbs need? The answer depends on a few factors, including the size and type of pot, the kind of soil, and the climate in your home.

However, most herbs need to be watered once a week. Allow the top inch of soil to dry out before watering again, and be sure to empty any water that collects in the saucer beneath the pot.

Overwatering is one of the most common mistakes made with indoor plants. If the leaves of your herbs are yellowing, it's an indication that they are getting too much water, while wilting leaves are a sign that they need more water.

When the soil is dry to the touch, this is a great indication that your plant needs watering, so be sure to check up on your plants regularly.

Understanding when to water your herbs is essential but also understanding how to water your herbs is just as important. If you want healthy herbs, you need to water them properly.

The best way to water indoor herbs is to use a mister or spray bottle. This will give the leaves a gentle shower, simulating rain, but be sure to mist the leaves evenly, getting both the top and bottom. You should also mist the soil, ensuring it is evenly moist but not soggy.

Water your herbs in the morning so they have time to dry before nightfall, which will help prevent mold and mildew growth. With a little trial and error, you'll soon get a feel for how often and how to water your indoor herbs.

Fertilization For Winter Herbs

Fertilizing your indoor herbs is vital to maintain a healthy plant. You can encourage growth by giving them the necessary nutrients and preventing problems like yellowing leaves or stunted growth.

When it comes to fertilizing your indoor herbs, there are a few things you need to take into account. The first is the type of plant you are growing. Some herbs, such as rosemary and oregano, are heavy feeders and will need more nutrient-rich soil. In contrast, thyme is more delicate and will do best in lighter soil.

Additionally, you will need to choose a fertilizer that is specifically designed for use with indoor plants. Many standard garden fertilizers can be too strong for indoor plants and may burn their roots, so a slow-release or liquid fertilizer is a better option for indoor plants.

Depending on the type of fertilizer you use, you may need to fertilize your indoor herb plants every few weeks or so.

If you use a liquid fertilizer, you can simply add it to the water when you water your plants. However, if you use a granular fertilizer, you will need to apply it directly to the soil, but be sure to follow the instructions on the package, as too much fertilizer can damage your plants.

In general, it is better to err on the side of caution and fertilize less often than more.

Choosing the right rosemary fertilizer is essential if you want to grow healthy plants. Organic options are generally the best, as they provide a slow release of nutrients that won't burn the roots.

However, some synthetic fertilizers can work well. Look for one high in nitrogen and phosphorus, as these two elements are essential for healthy growth.

You should also ensure that the fertilizer you choose is suitable for indoor use. Some brands contain salts that can build up over time and damage the roots of your plants.

When it comes to indoor thyme plants, the right fertilizer can make all the difference.

Thyme is a delicate plant that doesn't require a lot of nutrients, so using a fertilizer that is too strong can do more harm than good. A regular weak fertilizer solution is the best way to ensure that your thyme gets the nutrients without being overwhelmed.

When choosing a fertilizer for indoor thyme, look for a fertilizer that is high in nitrogen and specifically designed for use with herbs.

One of the best things you can do for your oregano plants is to give them the right fertilizer. Indoor oregano plants depend heavily on you for their nutrients, so choosing a fertilizer that will provide them with everything they need to prosper is essential.

Look for a fertilizer with a high phosphorus content, encouraging strong root growth. While a nitrogen-rich fertilizer will promote leaf growth. It would help if you also looked for a fertilizer containing micronutrients such as iron and magnesium, which are essential for healthy plant growth.

Lastly, choose a fertilizer specifically designed for indoor use, as this will help prevent any unwanted residuals from building up in your soil.

With a little trial and error followed by assistance from these guidelines, you will quickly find the perfect fertilizer practices that will ensure your herb plants stay healthy and thrive.

PROTECTING YOUR WINTER HERBS

One of the great things about growing herbs indoors is that plants are less prone to a number of threats, pests, and diseases. However, these threats aren't completely nullified, so it is still important to understand how to identify and prevent such threats from causing damage to our herb plants.

While some of the problems our herb plants may encounter result from our practices, such as overwatering or not providing the proper type of fertilization, the good news is that these problems can be resolved by simply tweaking and fine-tuning our practices.

Unfortunately, even the cleanest homes can provide a hospitable environment for pests such as aphids, whiteflies, and mealybugs.

These tiny creatures can quickly destroy an herb plant and are challenging to eliminate once they take hold. However, there are a few things that you can do to prevent pests from becoming a problem in the first place.

First, make sure that your plants are receiving enough light. Pests are attracted to weak and stressed plants, so healthy plants are less likely to be infested.

Second, regularly inspect your plants, and remove any pests you see as soon as possible. Third, choose pest-resistant varieties of plants whenever possible. By taking these simple precautions, you can help to keep your indoor herb garden free of pests.

HARVESTING WINTER HERBS

Growing herbs indoors can provide you with a fresh, year-round supply of flavorful harvest. But how do you harvest once your herbs mature and are ready?

The best time to harvest most herbs is in the morning after the dew has evaporated but before the day's heat sets in. Using sharp scissors or pruning shears, snip off individual stems, taking care not to damage the rest of the plant; this will help prevent the plant from becoming leggy and spindly.

You can give the plant a gentle haircut for leafy herbs like oregano, taking care not to remove more than one-third of the foliage. The key is to harvest and regularly trim, as this will encourage the plants to keep growing.

Each plant has its varied growth rate and maturing period, so it is essential to understand when each plant is due for harvest.

The maturity date for thyme is 70 days from when planted. Rosemary can be harvested 85 days from the planted date, whereas oregano can be harvested between 35-44 days from when planted.

Once you've harvested your herbs, it's important to store them in a cool, dry place out of direct sunlight to allow them to dry.

Alternatively, the herbs can be cut and placed in a single layer on a baking sheet. Once they have dried, the herbs can be stored in an airtight container in a cool, dark location or kept in the freezer for longer-term preservation. However, you choose to use them, harvesting your indoor herbs is a satisfying way to enjoy the fruits (or leaves) of your labor.

SAVING WINTER HERBS SEEDS

Now that we have harvested our rosemary oregano and thyme plants, you may wonder how to harvest the seeds for future cultivation. The good news is that it is relatively easy to do. The first step is to wait until the plant blooms.

Once the flowers begin to fade, they will turn into small seed pods. These pods should be lightly crushed to release the seeds. Next, spread the seeds on a sheet of paper and allow them to air dry for several days.

Once completely dry, you can store them in an airtight container until you are ready to use them. With a little patience and care, you can easily propagate herbs from seed and enjoy an abundance of flavor for years to come.

CHAPTER 6
GROWING YOUR WINTER GARLIC

There's something about garlic's sharp, pungent flavor that just makes food taste better. Whether used to add a kick to a soup, give some extra zing to a sauce, or used as a seasoning, garlic can make even the most mundane dish more delicious.

And it's not just the flavor that garlic adds to food - it's also said to have health benefits. It's been proven that garlic can help to boost the immune system, and it has even been used as a natural remedy for colds and flu.

Whether you're using it for its flavor or its health benefits, adding garlic to your vegetable harvest this winter will yield nothing but goodness in your kitchen and health.

THE RIGHT SOIL FOR GARLIC

Garlic is a frost-hardy plant that can be planted in late fall for a winter harvest. The key to successful garlic cultivation is choosing the right soil type.

Garlic prefers loose, well-drained soil with high organic content. If your soil is heavy or clay-like, consider amending it with compost or peat moss to improve drainage.

The best soil for growing garlic is rich and loamy, with good drainage. Sandy soil is also suitable as long as it is amended with organic matter to improve its water-retention capacity.

Garlic prefers neutral to slightly alkaline soil, with a pH between 6.5 and 7.5, so if your soil is on the acidic side, you may need to add some lime to raise the pH level.

When preparing the bed for planting, work in some well-rotted manure or compost to help improve the fertility and structure of the soil.

It's important to always test your garden soil, especially ground soil before using it to be sure it's healthy and meets the specified requirements.

Alternatively, there's the option to buy pre-made soil for growing garlic. Using this option may cut out some work for you; however, it is best practice to understand your garden's ins and outs and testing your soil is a great way to do so.

Like when growing any other vegetable plant, clean your garden soil beforehand and ensure it's free from pests, debris, and disease; doing so gives your plants the best possible chance of thriving.

Garlic Plant Diseases

Garlic is a beloved ingredient in cuisines worldwide, and it's no wonder why. This aromatic plant has a versatile flavor that can enhance both sweet and savory dishes.

Unfortunately, garlic is also susceptible to several diseases that can cause problems for home gardeners. Here are some of the most common garlic plant diseases:

Pythium root rot: Pythium root rot is caused by a water mold that attacks the roots of garlic plants. Symptoms include yellowing leaves, wilting, and stunted growth. The best way to prevent Pythium root rot is to plant garlic in well-drained soil and water only when necessary.

Fusarium wilt: Fusarium wilt is caused by a soil-borne fungus that infects the watering vessels of garlic plants. Symptoms include yellowing leaves, wilting, and stunted growth. The best way to prevent Fusarium wilt is to plant garlic in well-drained soil and water only when necessary.

Black rot: Black rot is caused by a fungus that attacks the leaves of garlic plants. Symptoms include black streaks on the leaves, wilting, and stunted growth.

The best way to prevent black rot is to plant garlic in well-drained soil and only water it when necessary. If you notice any symptoms of black rot, remove affected leaves from the plant immediately.

Downy mildew: Downy mildew is caused by a fungus that attacks the leaves of garlic plants. Symptoms include white powdery spots on the leaves, wilting, and stunted growth.

The best way to prevent downy mildew is to plant garlic in well-drained soil and water only when necessary. If you notice any symptoms of downy mildew, again remove affected leaves from the plant immediately.

Additionally, you can take extra measures to prevent these diseases from taking over your garlic patch. Start by planting disease-resistant varieties.

One big reason to use disease-resistant garlic varieties is that they help reduce the amount of garlic fungicides in the environment and your soil.

They also help reduce the time and money you have to spend on treatment, and because they're more likely to stay healthy in the first place, they tend to produce higher yields.

Make sure to get your garlic disease-resistant varieties from a reputable source to know you're getting high-quality, disease-resistant seeds.

As simple as it may sound, avoiding overcrowding and planting your plants too close. Overcrowded plants will cause plants to compete for limited resources like sunlight, water, and nutrients from the soil. This can lead to stunted growth, smaller bulbs, and an increased risk of disease and pests.

While these diseases are devastating for garlic crops, they can be prevented with proper care and attention.

HOW TO SOW GARLIC

Correct Season To Plant Garlic

One of the best times to plant garlic is in the fall, a few months before the first frost. This gives the garlic time to establish roots and develop a strong base before winter sets in.

This results in a more flavorful crop and ensures that the cloves are large and plump. In addition, fall-planted garlic is less likely to bolt or produce flower stalks in the spring.

The ideal time to plant garlic is September or October when the days are still warm, but the nights are starting to cool down.

Planting Needs And Requirements

To germinate garlic seeds, start by soaking them in water for a day or two days. Soaking the seeds will help them germinate faster by cutting down the time it takes for the shell to soften and the sprouting to begin.

You can do this with most seeds; however, it's beneficial with seeds that take longer to germinate. In warm water or chamomile tea (with no sugar, of course!), put your seeds inside and let them soak and soften for around a day or two.

You will then take the softened seeds and plant them in the moistened potting mix about half inch deep. Place the pots in a warm, sunny location and moisten the soil.

Between 8 to 10 days, you should see signs of growth. Remember to get the temperatures between 70 – 80 degrees Fahrenheit to ensure your seeds sprout successfully.

Once the seedlings are a few inches tall, thin them out and space them about 4 inches apart. With proper care, your garlic seedlings should thrive and produce healthy plants.

Spacing And Measurements

Now that your seedlings have been successfully established, it's time to move them into their new and permanent location; this can be in containers, raised beds, and traditional in-ground.

Understanding the right spacing and measurements for your plant plays a huge role in the success of your crops, so it's essential that this stage carried out correctly.

In terms of measurements, garlic plants should be spaced about 15-18 inches apart in rows 24-36 inches apart. This will ensure that the plants have enough space to develop and that the bulbs will have adequate air circulation, which is necessary for preventing disease.

Once planted, be sure to water your plants, ensuring to soil is moist but not soggy. Finally, it is essential to plant garlic in an area that receives full sun; this is at least six hours of sunlight per day.

This will ensure that the plants receive the warmth and light necessary for proper and healthy growth. By following these simple guidelines, you can be sure that your garlic plants will thrive and flourish in no time.

MAINTAINING YOUR GARLIC

Any garlic lover knows that there's nothing quite like the taste of freshly-grown garlic. However, growing your garlic can be a bit of a challenge. Giving your plants the necessary care is essential to produce a good harvest.

Maintenance can come in different forms, from under-standing how and when to prune your crops, watering schedules and requirements, fertilizing your plants, and much more.

In the following, we will be going through the importance and how to successfully maintain all aspects of your Garlic plants, ensuring they are on track to the freshest and ripest winter harvest.

Pruning And Thinning Your Garlic

If you want garlic that won't disappoint you at harvest time, pruning and thinning your plants is one of the most important things you will need to do.

By pruning, you encourage the plant to produce new growth, which is necessary for producing a large garlic bulb. The plant will eventually stop growing if you don't prune your garlic.

Thinning your garlic gives the individual cloves room to grow, ensuring that each one is plump and healthy. If you don't thin your garlic, the cloves will be small and shrivelled.

Now that we understand the importance of pruning and trimming our garlic plants, here are some guidelines for successfully doing so. First, you'll need to cut off any dead or dying leaves. Next, it is required to trim back any long or straggly leaves.

To prune your garlic plants, snip off the tops of the plants. This will encourage the plants to produce more bulbs.

To thin your garlic plants, dig up one plant for every six that remain. This will ensure that the remaining plants have enough space to grow properly, preventing stunted growth and competition for limited space and resources.

Additionally, when it comes to harvest, you'll be able to easily pull up the bulbs without damaging the surrounding plants.

It only takes a little bit of time and effort to prune and thin your garlic plants, and by doing so, you'll be rewarded with a bountiful harvest of healthy, delicious bulbs.

Watering Garlic

Watering garlic plants is a simple but critical task in ensuring a healthy crop. These hearty plants don't need a lot of water to thrive. Too much water can harm garlic, causing the bulbs to rot.

Unlike most plants, garlic benefits from a period of drought during the growing season. This stress forces the plant to put all its energy into developing large, flavorful bulbs.

As a general rule of thumb, garlic should be watered about once a week, giving the soil a good soaking until it is moist but not soggy.

Garlic plants only need about 1 inch of water per week. However, during especially hot or dry periods, you may need to water your garlic plants more frequently.

Stick your finger in the soil to check if your plants need water. If the soil is dry up to your first knuckle, it's time to water. However, be sure not to overwater; too much water can be just as damaging as too little. Waterlogged soil can lead to fungal diseases and cause garlic bulbs to rot.

The key is to keep the soil moist without over-watering it. One way to achieve this is to water early in the day, so the leaves have time to dry off before nightfall.

Another is to water at the base of the plant, rather than above, to avoid wetting the foliage. Watering garlic plants doesn't have to be complicated or time-consuming and by following these simple tips you will ensures your plants stay healthy and produce a bountiful harvest.

Fertilization For Garlic

Garlic plants are relatively easy to grow but require some care to ensure a good harvest. One crucial aspect of garlic care is fertilization. There are several types of fertilization that can be used for garlic plants.

One common method is to apply organic matter, such as compost or manure, around the plants; this helps to provide nutrients and improve soil structure.

Another option is to use chemical fertilizers, such as nitrogen, phosphorus, and potassium, where a balanced fertilizer with a ratio of 10-10-10 is ideal.

These can be applied in either granular or liquid form. Granular fertilizers are spread over the surface of the soil and then watered in, while liquid fertilizers are mixed with water and applied directly to the roots.

For both types of fertilizer, it is essential to follow the manufacturer's directions for application. Too much fertilizer can damage the roots and leaves of garlic plants.

Garlic plants also benefit from regular applications of mulch. Mulch helps to keep the soil moist and cool, which is ideal for garlic growth. It also helps to prevent weeds from competing with garlic for nutrients.

Organic mulches, such as wood chips or bark, are a good choice for garlic plants. Inorganic mulches, such as plastic sheeting, can also be used but should be removed before planting new garlic cloves in the fall.

PROTECTING YOUR GARLIC

Extreme Temperatures

Garlic is a tough plant that can tolerate a wide range of temperatures, but it does have its limits. Garlic plants generally prefer moderate temperatures between 30 – 50 degrees Fahrenheit and will wilt and die if the temperature gets too high or too low.

Extreme heat with temperatures reaching 80 degrees Fahrenheit can cause the garlic to stop growing, while extreme colds as low as 5 degrees Fahrenheit can cause garlic heads to die.

However, the good news is that garlic heads can regrow once temperatures have reached 40 degrees Fahrenheit.

That said, protecting garlic plants from extreme temperature swings is still vital. One way to do this is to water them regularly, which helps to regulate the soil temperature around the plants.

Additionally, mulching can help insulate the garlic from hot and cold weather. When mulching for extremely cool temperatures, be sure that your layers are 6 inches thick.

When it comes to the type of mulch to use to protect your plants, a variety of mulches can be used. In colder climates, straw or hay can insulate the plants and help prevent frost damage.

In warmer temperatures, wood chips or shredded leaves can help keep the soil cool and moist.

By following and utilizing the provided guidance, you can assure your garlic plants have all the tools to survive even the most extreme temperatures.

Protecting Winter Garlic From Pests

Garlic is a powerhouse of flavor and nutrition, but it's also beloved by many pests. If you're growing garlic, it's essential to be vigilant about protecting your plants from insect damage.

One of the most common pests that attack garlic is the bulb mite. These tiny spider-like creatures are barely visible to the naked eye, but they can cause significant problems for garlic plants.

They feast on the leaves of the plant, weakening the plant and making it more susceptible to disease.

Regular inspections of your garlic plants are essential to prevent bulb mites from getting a foothold in your garden. Look for tiny webs or eggs on the underside of leaves, and remove any affected leaves immediately.

Keep an eye out for other pests, such as aphids and white-flies. These insects can be controlled with various methods, including insecticidal soap, neem oil, and beneficial predators.

This is where it gets interesting; you may find that your garlic plants may not be as susceptible to pests as other vegetables you have grown or may be growing.

Why is this, you may ask? This is because garlic is also a powerful weapon against pests; whether dealing with pesky insects or hungry rodents, just a few cloves of garlic are enough to keep them at bay.

When planted in your garden, the pungent smell of garlic will discourage many common pests, such as aphids, from entering your garden.

Rodents such as mice and rats are also deterred. So by simply following these simple tips, you can keep your garlic plants healthy and free from pests.

HARVESTING WINTER GARLIC

Enjoying fresh garlic all winter is one of the best things about having a garlic crop. But to have a successful harvest, it's essential to know when to start harvesting garlic.

Garlic plants usually take 180 – 210 days to harvest from seeds to full maturity. Garlic should generally be harvested when the bottom two leaves have turned brown.

However, if you live in an area with a short growing season, it's best to harvest garlic as soon as the leaves begin to turn brown. This will help ensure that your garlic doesn't rot before it has a chance to cure.

When harvesting garlic, dig up the entire plant, including the root system. Cut off the top of the plant about 2 inches from the bulb, then brush away any excess dirt.

Hang the plants upside down in a cool, dark place for about two weeks to allow the bulbs to cure. Once they're cured, trim off the roots and store the bulbs in a cool, dry place. Once harvested, the garlic can be stored in a cool, dry place for several months.

Additionally, when choosing which bulbs to store, look for those that are large and have well-formed cloves, and avoid storing any bulbs that are damaged or show signs of rot.

With proper care, your stored garlic should last until springtime.

SAVING GARLIC SEEDS

Harvesting garlic seeds is a simple process that can be done in just a few steps. First, wait until the foliage of the garlic plant begins to yellow and die back. This usually occurs in late summer or early fall.

Next, carefully dig up the bulbs and separate them into individual cloves. Each clove will contain a small amount of garlic seed. Simply break open the clove and remove the seeds. Once the seeds are exposed, they can be dried in a cool, dark place.

Once completely dry, store them in an airtight container in a cool, dark place until you're ready to plant them. So with patience and care, you can successfully harvest garlic seeds and enjoy fresh garlic for years to come.

CHAPTER 7
GROWING YOUR
WINTER BROCCOLI

There's something about broccoli that makes it so versatile. Whether using it as a main ingredient or as a supporting player, it always manages to make its presence felt.

Perhaps it's the way it holds its shape when cooked, or maybe it's the slightly nutty flavor that goes so well with so many other ingredients. Aside from the flavourful taste of broccoli, there are many other benefits to growing your own broccoli.

For one, you can be sure that the quality of the broccoli is high since you have control over how it is grown. Additionally, it is packed with vitamins and minerals, and its green color indicates that it is high in chlorophyll, which has numerous health benefits.

Whatever the reason, broccoli is a popular and great choice of vegetable to add to your winter harvest so let's get right into it.

THE RIGHT SOIL FOR BROCCOLI

Broccoli is a winter crop that thrives in cool weather, frosty nights and is a relatively easy crop to grow, however it does have some specific soil requirements. To produce a bountiful harvest of this cruciferous vegetable, gardeners must plant their seeds in the correct soil type.

The ideal soil for winter broccoli is rich in organic matter, well-drained, and slightly acidic, with a pH level between 6.0 and 6.8. With these conditions, gardeners can expect their plants to thrive and produce a bountiful harvest.

In addition to providing the right nutrients, the soil should also be loose enough to allow the roots to spread without restraint.

Lastly, it is essential to ensure the soil is well-drained, as waterlogged roots can lead to rot and fungal diseases.

Broccoli Plant Diseases

There are several diseases that can affect broccoli plants. One of the most common is black rot, which is caused by a fungus. This disease causes the leaves of the plant to turn yellow and then black and can also cause the stems to rot.

Another disease that can affect broccoli plants is downy mildew, also caused by a fungus. This disease causes the leaves to develop gray or white spots; eventually, the leaves will turn brown and die. In addition, downy mildew can also cause the plant's stems to become weak and brittle.

Finally, Cercospora leaf spot is another disease that can affect broccoli plants. This disease causes small, dark spots on the plant's leaves, eventually leading to the leaves turning yellow and dying. Another common issue is club root, which causes the roots to swell and deform. This disease is typically caused by soil that is too alkaline, so it's essential to test your soil before planting.

Luckily, there are several ways to prevent these diseases from occurring, such as using diseases resistant varieties of broccoli, providing adequate plant ventilation, and keeping the foliage dry. By ensuring your plants are getting enough drainage, you are actively preventing such diseases from occurring.

HOW TO SOW BROCCOLI

Correct Season To Plant Broccoli

The best time to plant broccoli for a winter harvest is in the late summer or early fall after the summer heat has passed but before the first frost. This ensures that the plants have enough time to mature and produce a good crop before the cold weather sets in.

Broccoli is a cool-weather crop that does not do well in hot, dry conditions. It is also relatively sensitive to frost, so it is essential to plant it early enough in the season that it will have time to mature before the first frost hits.

If you plant broccoli too late in the season, you may end up with a smaller, less bountiful crop. But if you plant it right, you can enjoy fresh, healthy broccoli all winter. When choosing a location for your broccoli plants, choose a spot with plenty of sunlight. Broccoli thrives in sunny locations and will produce more heads if grown in a sunny spot.

Planting Needs And Requirements

The process of germinating broccoli seeds is not particularly complicated, but a few key steps must be followed for the seeds to sprout successfully. First, the seeds should be soaked in water for 24 hours. This will help to soften the hard outer shell and allow the seedling to emerge more quickly.

After soaking, you'll need to fill your peat pots or seedling tray with potting mix ready for seeds to be planted in. Plant each about an inch deep in the soil, where seeds should be planted 6 inches apart if you intend to germinate multiple seeds in a single container.

Once the seeds are in the soil, cover them with a thin layer of vermiculite or sand. Place the tray in a warm location (around 70 degrees Fahrenheit is ideal) and moisten the soil. Your seeds should start to germinate within 7-10 days, where they will reach heights of 4-6 inches tall. At this point, you'll need to thin out the seedlings so that they have enough space to grow.

Spacing And Measurements

Now that your seedlings are established, it's time to relocate them to their new and permanent location. Whether you decide to grow your broccoli in-ground, in containers, or in raised beds, the principle for spacing and measurement stands the same for each method.

When planting broccoli seedlings, it is vital to consider spacing and measurements. Each seedling plant should be spaced 18-24 inches apart, with rows 24-36 inches apart.

It's also important to remember that when transplanting, make sure that the plant's roots are not disturbed and that the plant is firmly planted at the same depth it was growing previously.

As previously mentioned, it is vital to ensure that the seedlings are placed in an area that receives at least six hours of sunlight per day. Once the seedlings are in place, they should be watered thoroughly and regularly monitored to ensure the soil is moist but not soggy.

With proper care, your broccoli seedlings will thrive and produce a bountiful harvest in no time.

MAINTAINING YOUR BROCCOLI

Gardeners know that broccoli is a hardy plant that can withstand a fair amount of challenges and still produce delicious, nutritious heads of broccoli. However, there are a few things you can do to ensure that your broccoli plants remain healthy and productive.

To keep your broccoli plants healthy, it is essential to water them regularly, fertilize them regularly and thin them regularly. Doing so creates the necessary tools to ensure they thrive, providing the freshest and ripest produce for your winter harvest.

Pruning And Thinning Your Broccoli

Pruning and thinning your broccoli plants can seem daunting, but it's pretty simple, and they serve an essential purpose. First, you'll need to remove any dead or yellow leaves.

Grab a sharp knife or gardening shears and cut the leaves away from the stem. Next, you'll need to thin out the plants. This means removing some of the smaller, weaker plants so that the remaining plants have more space to grow and not compete for nutrients and water.

Again, use a sharp knife or gardening shears to carefully remove the plants you want to thin out. Finally, prune the plants by trimming away any excess growth. This will help encourage the plants to grow more evenly and produce larger heads of broccoli. At the same time, pruning will help avoid overcrowding; as a result, this helps in the prevention of pests and diseases infection your plants.

Watering Broccoli

When watering broccoli plants, the key is to strike a balance. Water them too little, and the plants will wilt and become stressed; overwater them, and the plants may develop fungal diseases.

Therefore, it is crucial to water broccoli plants regularly, ensuring the soil stays moist but not soggy. One way to achieve this is to water in the morning so that the plants have time to absorb the water before nightfall.

This will minimize the risk of fungal diseases and provide the plants with the moisture they need to produce delicious heads of broccoli.

The best way to water broccoli is to give the plants a deep soaking once a week. This will encourage the roots to grow deep into the soil, leading to stronger plants that are better able to resist drought.

When watering, it is also important to apply the water slowly so that it has a chance to seep down to the roots.

That said, it is essential to factor in how the weather can affect the watering schedule of your broccoli plants. After heavy rain, it's advised to pause watering your plants for a week to ensure they are not over-saturated.

Containers and soil with good drainage will also help with preventing waterlogging in your plants, so be sure to select the right type for your broccoli plants from the very start. Following these simple tips will ensure your broccoli plants receive the moisture they need to thrive.

Fertilization For Broccoli

Broccoli is a nutrient-rich vegetable that can be valuable to any diet. To grow healthy broccoli plants, it is crucial to provide them with the right mix of nutrients. One way to do this is through fertilization.

When fertilizer is added to the soil, it helps to replenish essential nutrients that may have been depleted by previous growth. This makes the soil more fertile and able to support healthy plant growth.

Many different types of fertilizer are available, so it is important to choose one specifically designed for broccoli plants.

One type of fertilizer that can be used on broccoli plants is compost. This is created by breaking down organic matter, such as food scraps and leaves, into a rich, loose material full of nutrients.

Compost can be added to the soil around broccoli plants or used as a mulch to help retain moisture and prevent weeds.

Another type of fertilizer that can be used on broccoli is manure. This is usually made from cow or horse manure and is high in nitrogen and other essential nutrients.

Manure can be applied to the soil around broccoli plants or used as a compost tea. This is made by soaking manure in water and then using the liquid to water the plants.

Either way, manure can provide a boost of nutrition that helps broccoli plants to grow strong and healthy.

Finally, there are chemical fertilizers, which are made from synthetic chemicals. Chemical fertilizers can quickly boost nutrients to plants, but they can also cause environmental damage if they are not used carefully.

For this reason, many gardeners prefer to use organic fertilizers instead of chemical ones.

As a whole, it's recommended to start fertilizing your plant around three weeks after they have been transplanted into its new location, using a low in nitrogen formula such as 5-10-10.

PROTECTING YOUR BROCCOLI

Extreme Temperatures

Broccoli is a tough plant that can withstand hot and cold temperatures. However, the plant is sensitive to extreme temperatures where irreversible damage can occur.

Broccoli plants can survive temperatures between 30 – 85 degrees Fahrenheit; however, they thrive by producing the best quality heads within temperatures of 60 - 70 degrees Fahrenheit.

When exposed to temperatures below 30 degrees Fahrenheit, the water inside the broccoli cells will freeze, causing stunted growth. This damage is often irreversible and can result in misshapen or discolored heads of broccoli.

Additionally, temperatures above 85 degrees Fahrenheit will cause the plant to seed, producing small yellow flowers instead of the large green heads typically harvested.

As a result, it is essential to monitor the temperature when growing broccoli to ensure that the plants produce the desired results.

Protect Broccoli From Pests

Broccoli is a hardy plant that can withstand a fair amount of challenges, but even this tough veggie has its limits. Unfortunately, broccoli plants are often subject to attack by pests, which can quickly decimate an entire crop.

Here are some tips for protecting your plants from these ravenous critters.

One of the most effective ways to protect your broccoli plants is to create a physical barrier. Fencing off your garden with chicken wire or another type of mesh can help to keep out larger pests like rabbits and deer. You can also use floating row covers to keep out smaller insects.

In addition to excluding pests, it's also essential to identify and remove any potential food sources. This means keeping your garden free of weeds, which can harbor aphids and other harmful insects.

It's also important to promptly remove any infested leaves or stems, as these can provide a meal for passing pests.

Attracting beneficial insects to your garden can help keep the pest population in check. Ladybugs, for example, feed on aphids, while lacewings devour both aphids and mites.

By providing a habitat for these helpful creatures, you can encourage them to stick around and help keep your broccoli plants healthy and pest-free.

Finally, planting companion plants is a great way to repel pests. For example, basil helps keep aphids away, while sage helps control caterpillars.

You can also discourage pests by making your own DIY organic pest spray. Simply mix water and organic soap in a spray bottle and use it to target specific areas of infestation.

While implementing the previously advised practices, it is essential to regularly check your plants for signs of infestation to catch any problems early.

Look for holes in leaves or abnormal chewing damage, and look for common pests such as aphids, Japanese beetles, and caterpillars. If you see any pests on your plants, immediately remove them by hand or with a blast of water from the hose.

Following these simple steps can keep your broccoli plants healthy and safe from harm.

HARVESTING WINTER BROCCOLI

When harvesting broccoli, the main goal is to cut the central head before it flowers. Once the head is cut, the plant will continue to produce small side shoots that can be harvested throughout the winter season.

Broccoli is typically ready to harvest 60-80 days after planting. To determine if the head is ready to harvest, look for tight clusters of green florets about 4-6 inches in diameter. The stem should be at least 6 inches long.

If the head is left on the plant for too long, it will begin to flower, making the stems tough and the florets bitter. When harvesting broccoli, use a sharp knife or garden shears to avoid damaging the plant.

Cut the stem about 2 inches below the floret cluster and rinse the broccoli under cool water. Once harvested you can store your broccoli in an airtight container in the refrigerator for up to one week.

Now you can enjoy your freshly harvested broccoli in various recipes and dishes!

SAVING WINTER BROCCOLI SEEDS

When harvesting seeds from your broccoli plants, there are a few things to keep in mind. First, wait until the plant produces flowers. Once the flowers begin to wilt and turn brown, that's a sign that the seeds are ripening.

Cut off the flower head and place it in a paper bag. Tie the bag shut and leave it in a warm, dry place for a few weeks. Once the seeds are dry, they can be removed from the flower head and stored in an airtight container with a life span of up to 3 years.

With just a little care, you can easily harvest seeds from your broccoli plants and save them for next year's garden.

CHAPTER 8
GROWING YOUR WINTER LETTUCE

L ettuces are one of the most popular vegetables in the world, and for a good reason. Lettuces are versatile greens used in various dishes, from salads and sandwiches to fine cuisines; the list is endless.

Growing your lettuce is a great way to get fresh, healthy greens without relying on the grocery store. Plus, it's a fun and easy way to get started with gardening. Lettuce is a cool-weather crop, so it can be one of the first things you plant in the spring.

There are wide varieties of lettuce, from crisp iceberg to delicate butterhead. With so many choices, you're sure to find a type you enjoy eating, and since lettuce grows quickly, you'll be able to harvest your homegrown greens in no time.

So why not give it a try? The crunchy, crispy, and nutritious vegetable is one of the best additions to any winter harvest.

THE RIGHT SOIL FOR LETTUCE

Starting with the right soil is essential to produce a bountiful crop of lettuce. The soil should be loose and loamy, with a good balance of organic matter.

It should also be well-drained, as lettuces will not do well in soggy conditions. In terms of pH, lettuces prefer slightly acidic soil, with a pH between 6.0 and 6.5. The best way to ensure that your soil has the right conditions is to conduct a soil test.

This will give you an accurate picture of the nutrient levels in your soil and help you make any necessary adjustments. With the right soil in place, you will be well on your way to growing a delicious crop of lettuces.

Lettuce Plant Diseases

Lettuce is a popular leafy green vegetable that is unfortunately susceptible to several diseases that can cause extensive damage to crops.

One of the most common lettuce diseases is downy mildew. This pathogen thrives in cool, moist conditions and can quickly spread through fields, leading to widespread crop loss.

Symptoms of downy mildew include yellow or brown spots on the leaves, along with a white or gray mold that forms on the underside of the leaves.

To control downy mildew, gardeners often use fungicides, but these products must be applied at the right time and in the right amount to be effective.

Another common lettuce disease is bacterial leaf spots. This pathogen thrives in warm, humid conditions and spreads quickly through fields.

Symptoms of bacterial leaf spots include small, dark spots on the leaves and yellowing and wilting. Gardeners often use copper-based fungicides to control this disease, but as with downy mildew, timing is critical for these products to be effective.

If you notice any of these symptoms, remove the affected leaves and dispose of them to prevent the disease from spreading.

Also, prevention methods can be implemented to reduce the likelihood of your plants being attacked and infected. Disease-resistant varieties are preferred when sourcing lettuce seeds, as they have been bred to resist common plant diseases, ensuring your plants can grow into healthy and strong harvests.

Keeping your garden clean by removing dead leaves and debris before planting and at the end of the season will help reduce the amount of decaying matter that can harbor diseases over winter.

Watering early in the day is an effective way to prevent disease occurrence. Watering in the morning gives the plants time to dry off before nightfall when damp conditions favor disease development.

Avoid overhead watering as this can wet the leaves, providing an ideal environment for fungal diseases to take hold. Instead, water at the base of the plants using a soaker hose or drip irrigation system.

Following these tips can help prevent lettuce plant diseases and enjoy a bountiful harvest of crisp, healthy greens.

HOW TO SOW LETTUCE

Correct Season To Plant Lettuce

The best time to plant lettuce for a winter harvest is early fall. You can enjoy fresh greens all winter long by planting seeds in September or October. Lettuce is a cool-weather crop that grows best in temperatures between 60 and 65 degrees Fahrenheit.

To prevent the plants from bolting—or going to seed—during the warmer months, give them plenty of water and shade. Lettuce generally requires at least six hours sunlight each day to grow properly.

However, lettuce can be planted under taller crops, such as tomatoes or corn, to avoid bolting in hotter temperatures. Alternatively, you can use a parasol or other type of shading structure.

Keep in mind that lettuce will still need some sunlight for photosynthesis, so don't place it in complete darkness. The leaves will become pale and spindly if you provide too much shade.

Planting Needs And Requirements

Germinating seeds into a seedling is a straightforward process preferred to be carried out indoors. By doing so, the optimum environment can be easily simulated to ensure your seeds get the best possible start in their growing journey.

To germinate, you'll need a pot or container with drainage holes, some potting mix, and lettuce seeds. Fill the pot with the seed-starting mix, then sprinkle the lettuce seeds on top.

Gently press the seeds into the mix, covering them with half a inch of soil, mist them lightly, ensuring that they are moist but not soggy, and then place them in a warm spot.

The seeds should start germinating in 5-10 days when tiny seedlings poke through the soil's surface. Once seedlings have sprouted, thin them, so they're about 6 inches apart.

Spacing And Measurements

With the seedling now ready to be sown in their permanent location, it's crucial to understand the required spacing and measurements to ensure the plants are not overcrowded and competing for nutrients.

Whether you're choosing to grow in containers, raised beds, or in-ground gardens, the following guidelines can be used to ensure your plants thrive.

When sowing the seedlings, loosen the soil with a hoe or tiller and sow the seedlings about half an inch deep in the soil. The recommended space for planting lettuce is 10-12 inches apart in the row, with 18-24 inches between rows.

This will give the plants plenty of room to mature and prevent overcrowding. When it comes to measurements, lettuces are typically 12-18 inches tall and 6-12 inches wide.

Lettuce plants need at least six hours of sunlight per day, so choose a spot in your garden that gets plenty of sun in the morning but is shaded from the afternoon heat.

MAINTAINING YOUR LETTUCE

Winter lettuce is one of the best ways to get greens during the colder months. But what happens when the lettuce starts to yellow and wilt? Don't despair! With a little care, you can keep your winter lettuce healthy and delicious all season long.

Pruning And Thinning Your Lettuce

Lettuce is a fast-growing crop that can be harvested just 50 days after planting. To ensure a steady supply of fresh leaves, it is important to prune and thin your lettuce plants regularly.

Pruning involves cutting off the plant's outer leaves, while thinning means removing entire plants to allow the remaining ones more room to grow. Pruning and thinning should be done when the plants are young and tender.

Here are some tips on how to prune and thin your lettuce.

To prune, use sharp shears or a knife to cut away the outer leaves, being careful not to damage the inner leaves or stem. You can also remove any damaged or yellowed leaves. Pruning encourages the plant to produce more leaves, so do it every week or two throughout the growing season.

Thinning should be done when the plants are about 4 inches tall. Use shears or a knife to carefully remove entire plants, taking care not to damage the roots of the remaining plants.

Thinning allows the remaining plants more room to grow and prevents overcrowding. Do it every few weeks throughout the growing season.

Watering Lettuce

Water is essential for all plants, but it is especially important for lettuce. These leafy greens comprise up to 95% water, so they rely on a steady supply to stay hydrated. Lettuce plants should be watered regularly, and the frequency will depend on factors such as soil type, weather, and growth stage.

Generally, it is best to water lettuce early in the day, so the leaves have time to dry before nightfall. Wet leaves are more susceptible to fungal diseases, so it is crucial to let them dry before the evening.

The amount of water required will also vary depending on these factors, but as a general rule, lettuces should be given enough water to keep the soil moist but not saturated.

Lettuce plants need about 1-2 inches of water per week from rainfall or irrigation. Be sure to avoid overwatering as it can lead to root rot and other problems, so it is essential to strike a balance. Following these guidelines ensures that your lettuce plants stay healthy and hydrated all season long.

Fertilization For Lettuce

Lettuce is a garden favorite for many home growers because of its easy care and versatility in the kitchen. While lettuce is not a heavy feeder, it does benefit from regular fertilization to produce the best results.

A fertilizer high in nitrogen will encourage foliage growth, while one higher in phosphorus will promote root development. For a well-rounded diet, look for a fertilizer with an NPK ratio of 5-10-5 or 6-12-6.

Apply the fertilizer according to the manufacturer's directions, generally every two to four weeks during the growing season. Side dressings of compost or aged manure can also be beneficial, especially if your lettuce is growing in containers.

These organic additions help improve drainage while providing nutrients that slow-release fertilizers may lack.

PROTECTING YOUR LETTUCES

Extreme Temperatures

Lettuce plants are susceptible to temperature changes and can be easily killed by extreme heat or cold. In warm weather, lettuce will quickly bolt, sending up a flower stalk and producing bitter-tasting leaves.

If the temperatures get too hot, reaching levels past 85 degrees Fahrenheit, leaves will wilt, and the plant will eventually die. In cool weather, lettuce will produce sweeter-tasting leaves, but if the temperatures dips too low, hitting levels of 25 degrees Fahrenheit and below, the plants will go into shock and may not recover.

As a result, it is crucial to ensure your plants are growing within the temperatures of 60 – 65 degrees Fahrenheit, where careful monitoring is required ensuring they remain healthy and productive.

In order to protect lettuce plants from extreme temperatures, it is important to take a few precautions. Firstly, it is important to choose a variety of lettuce resistant to heat and cold.

Secondly, it is important to water the plants regularly, as this will help to keep the roots cool. Thirdly, it is essential to mulch the plants, as this will help insulate them from heat and cold.

Finally, it is important to ensure that the plants are in direct sunlight for the required time and temperature, as this can cause the leaves to scorch.

Taking these simple precautions can help ensure that your lettuce plants remain healthy and productive despite extreme temperatures.

Protect Lettuce From Pests

Due to their highly nutritious leaves, lettuce plants are a common target of pests. Common garden pests, such as aphids, caterpillars, and slugs, can cause extensive damage to the plant and may even spread disease.

To protect lettuce plants from pests, it is essential to take preventative measures. Thankfully, there are several things that gardeners can do to protect their lettuce plants from pests.

To protect your lettuce plants from pests, it is necessary to inspect them regularly and take action if you see any signs of infestation.

Aphids and a variety of other problems can be controlled with insecticidal soap; this will eliminate any bugs currently feeding on the plants and help deter future attacks, while caterpillars can be picked off by hand. Diatomaceous earth or copper tape is also a great way to deter earwigs and slugs.

Choosing pest-resistant varieties of lettuce whenever possible is an effective prevention strategy while at the same time consistently keeping your garden clean and free of debris with good weed management.

Pests are known to use these locations as hiding spots, so the fewer hiding spots there are, the safer your lettuce plants are. Additionally, it is essential to inspect the plant regularly for signs of infestation.

If any pests are found, they should be removed immediately. By taking these simple steps, you can help to ensure that your lettuce plants stay healthy and free of pests.

HARVESTING LETTUCE

Lettuces usually take between 50 -75 days to harvest once planted. You could easily ruin your harvest if you are unaware of how quickly lettuces grow or aren't keeping track of the timeline.

Harvesting of lettuces is a straightforward process with minimal steps. When the leaves are crisp and green, it is time to harvest. Using a sharp knife, cut the leaves close to the base of the plant, but be sure to leave some of the leaves intact so the plant can continue to grow.

It's as simple as that; your lettuce plants are now ready to be washed and stored.

Lettuce can be stored in a refrigerator for up to a week or frozen for longer-term storage. To freeze lettuce, wash and dry the leaves, then chop them into smaller pieces.

Spread the chopped lettuce on a baking sheet and place it in the freezer. Once frozen, transfer the lettuce to a sealable bag or container; your lettuces can last up to several months.

SAVING LETTUCE SEEDS

When the time comes to harvest seeds from lettuce plants, gardeners have a few different options. One option is to allow the plants to bolt or produce a flower stalk.

Once the flowers have bloomed and begun to produce seeds, the stalks can be cut, and the seed heads can be dried in a cool, dark place.

Once the seed heads are completely dry, the seeds can be separated from the chaff and stored for future use. Another option is to cut the lettuce heads when they are still in the rosette stage. The heads can then be hung upside down in a cool, dark place until the leaves have withered and the seed heads are dry.

Again, the seeds can then be separated from the chaff and stored. Whichever method you choose, harvesting seed from lettuce plants is a simple process that will give you a sustainable supply of seeds for future planting.

CHAPTER 9
GLOSSARY

Acidic

Something that forms or becomes acid and has a pH of less than 7.

Aeration

The act of circulating air through a garden, soil, and plants.

Aged manure

Old manure that has matured through a long period by letting it sit in a container.

Alkaline

Something that contains alkali and has a pH above 7.

Aphids

Tiny insects which consume the liquid plants produce, such as sap.

Bacteria

A microorganism that causes disease and, at other times, improves the well-being of an organism.

Biodegradable

Something that can decompose into the soil and not harm the soil or other living organisms in it.

Bolting

When vegetable crops prematurely run to seed, usually making them unusable

Blunt

Something that is not sharp but softer around its edges and unable to penetrate through something.

Blanch

A method for growing vegetables. A condition in which a plant's young shoots are covered to block light, preventing photosynthesis and the production of chlorophyll, leaving them pale in color.

Bulb

A plant's fruit or organ grows in soil right above its roots and is typically edible when it's a vegetable plant.

Bushy

Something that is overgrown or grows to be dense, big, and has lots of leaves.

Cabbage loopers

An insect or moth tends to be found crawling and laying eggs on cabbages. This insect is a cabbage pest that destroys crops.

Calcium carbonate

Insoluble chalk is natural and white. This is also called ground limestone.

Collar

A round object is used to cuff the base of a plant to protect it from pests such as worms and maggots.

Compaction

The compression of soil particles removes air pockets and hardens the soil. It is considered harmful when gardening and if you want to achieve successful results.

Companion planting

Planting two or more plants next to each other and is protective of each other to avoid disease and pests. It can improve harvest results and improve growth.

Compost

A combination of biodegradable plants, objects, or waste that has been mixed to rot and build up nutrients necessary to soil health and fertility.

Container garden

A garden of plants grown in a pot that holds soil.

Crop Rotation

Planting various crops in succession on the same piece of land helps to improve soil health, maximise nutrients, and reduce pest and weed pressure. This practise is known as crop rotation.

Cutworms

A damaging and destructive moth larva is a vegetable pest found in soil and on plants.

Debris

Remains or objects in the soil, such as rocks and previously dead crops, need to be removed to maintain the health of your garden.

Drainage

The process by which liquids or water is expelled from something, such as soil.

Drilling tractor

A gardening sowing machine that drills holes into the ground and helps a gardener avoid manual soil drilling to plant his plants.

Ecosystem

Different biological organisms interact with each other to maintain an environment.

Evaporation

Water that turns into vapor.

Fertile Soil

Soil that is healthy enough to give plants all nutrients they need to grow successfully until harvest.

Fertilization

Making soil fertile through the use of fertilizers.

Frost

Ice crystals can form on plants when temperatures are freezing or too cold.

Frost Cloth

A covering made of insulation that is positioned over plants, shrubs, trees, and crops to shield them from frost, wind, and chilly weather.

Fungus

Living organisms feed on other living organisms and create mold or discolored plants when present. They can destroy plants and cause disease.

Germinate

When a plant starts to grow out of a shell and form shoots or leaves.

Harvest

A collection of mature and ripe plants and their fruit. It's when your plants have matured and you collect them from their stems.

Heart rate

How fast or slow are your heartbeats. It's a number or calculation which determines the heart's speed.

Humus

Decomposed organic matter consists of soil and compost.

Hybrid seed

Seeds have been altered and are offspring of two different types of seed varieties of the same plant.

Mesh

A material you lace over your garden plants that protects them from insects and pests.

Minerals

Substances are naturally occurring and are needed to produce fertile soil and healthy plants.

Moisture

Dampness is caused by diffused water or liquid.

Mulch

Decayed matter, such as compost, is placed on the soil's surface to lock moisture in or protect the soil from harsh weather conditions.

Nitrogen

A nutrient is needed to give plants their green color and healthy leaves.

Nutrients

Elements that feed plants the necessary food they need to grow.

Organic matter

Decomposed humus is in the soil and is essential in growing healthy vegetables.

Organic produce

Food that has been made or grown without the use of chemical alterations.

Pesticides

Organic or chemical substances kill or repel insects and other pests from a garden.

Pests

Living organisms are destructive to a garden and need to be repelled or prevented from reaching plants.

pH

A chemistry figure which communicates a scale of alkalinity or acidity. It helps you know how alkaline or acidic soil is.

Phosphate

Phosphoric acid is a salt needed for the soil's health.

Potassium

It is a nutrient that helps plants grow and is essential in their life cycle.

Pruning

Maintain a garden by cutting or trimming dead or potentially unwanted parts of a plant.

Roots

The bottom stingy and firm bits of a plant grow and stretch into the soil. They absorb the nutrients and water for a plant's needs.

Seedling

A small and recently germinated plant that is ready to be planted.

Soggy

A mushy, soft, and overly damp area such as soil.

Soilless

Matter which seeds can be grown in and is an alternative to soil.

Sowing

The act of planting, drilling, or scattering a seed onto or into the soil to grow.

Sprout

When a plant produces its first shoots or leaves.

Stem

The structure of a plant that supports all its branches, leaves, and fruit.

Suckers

Plant suckers are vigorous vertical growth originating from a plant's root system or lower main stem.

Thinning

Separating seedlings clumped together or removing some overcrowded plants from the soil to space out your garden to give others the chance of growing properly.

Transplanting

When you take a plant from one soil, area, or tray into another area or garden, this is also known as replanting it into another space.

ACKNOWLEDGEMENTS

Without the knowledge, experience, and commitment of our team at Green Roots, this book would not be possible.

We appreciate your contributions to this book, Charles Craig, Annie Hayford, Jessica Reid, Adam Spencer, and Nicole Robinson. Your dedication to making a difference in people's lives and developing this gardening community is unmatched.

This book is the product of more than 20 years' worth of collective expertise, experience, insight, and passion in the gardening field. We are all thrilled to have been able to create this body of work, to help, and to be used as a tool worldwide for gardeners of all levels of experience.

"Gardening is not just a hobby, but a way of life" - **(Green Roots 2022)**

AFTERWORD

There is no denying the benefits of starting your own garden! It genuinely has the power to change your life in ways you could never have imagined.

Your overall well-being can flourish, and your health can get better. If gardening does not have an immediate impact on yourself, we can assure you that it will make some aspects of your life better in the long run.

Why is Green Roots so sure of this? It's in science, after all! The therapeutic nature of gardening as a hobby and pastime has consistently demonstrated this. We would be able to tell stories after stories about how gardening has benefited us over the years and how it has personally impacted our lives.

Most importantly, the group of people we work with allows us to directly witness how gardening affects other people. Their lives are changed; they have a better outlook on life and feel better.

We took on the challenge of writing this book to dispel the myth that growing vegetables requires conventional space, tools, and equipment, all of which can be expensive.

Not only has gardening been made to appear difficult, but the various books and guides written to "make it easy" continue to fall short.

This book is intended to be simple to read, understand, and refer to whenever you face a gardening challenge. It's written in plain English to dispel the myth that gardening is all about fancy jargon and sounding like an "expert."

Yes, it's great to become an expert in this amazing world of gardening, especially when you can help others. However, being an expert would be useless if others cannot understand the knowledge and experience you possess and if your "tips and tricks" cannot be put into practice.

This book has taught and gone in depth on the fundamentals of garden. While it may only cover a few common vegetables and herbs for winter harvest, the information it imparts can easily apply to any other vegetable you might want to grow during this season. This information is exceptionally timeless in addition to being valuable.

Whether you are new to gardening or have been at it for decades, this book will serve as a point of reference. The basics of gardening don't change, so you'll be able to use this book for years. You can look back decades from now and still grasp how it's done.

With that being said, here are some great and key takeaways:

Types of Gardens

You are now aware that there are numerous options when it comes to the types of gardens. Even if you don't have enough yard space to begin a garden, you can start in containers and improvise as needed. You discovered that, while this is possible, containers may result in unfavorable harvest results for some plants that require deep roots.

You now thoroughly understand the benefits and drawbacks of each of the three types of gardens: container gardens, raised bed gardens, and traditional in-ground gardens.

Preparing the Soil

When starting a garden, one of the first things most new gardeners overlook is their soil. They accomplish this by being naive and simply purchasing compost and fertilizer without caring about or researching their soil.

However, you now understand the significance of knowing the type of soil you have, as soil and fertility are critical in a plant's ability to grow and produce as much yield as possible. You learned how to prepare, improve, maintain, and protect your soil in various ways.

Deciding What to Grow

Many beginners' gardeners purchase seeds and begin planting without first considering their "why" for starting the garden. This book helps you to decide the best types of vegetables suited to your needs and lifestyle .

Why spend time on a vegetable that won't make the most significant difference in your life? Unless you are gardening for a cause greater than yourself, choosing what vegetable to grow will be determined by your very own personal needs and no one else's.

Sowing Techniques

You discovered that sowing methods and techniques differ depending on the type of garden you want to plant and the size you want it to be.

This book has provided a solid understanding of the techniques and why they would or would not work in your garden. Each sowing technique is unique, but they can all be used in various situations.

This knowledge will assist you in avoiding time-consuming errors and, worse, financial loss due to incorrect sowing practices.

Growing Your Winter Vegetables

The biggest and most important thing you learned in this book is found in each vegetable planting guide for onions, peas, Brussels sprouts, winter herbs (rosemary, oregano, and thyme), garlic, broccoli, and lettuce.

With the in-depth guidance provided on each vegetable, you can now take actionable and confident steps from germinating your seeds all the way through to harvesting. As a result, you can expect the freshest and ripest vegetables this winter harvest.

The straightforward nature of this book, its advice and instructions will help any novice gardener thrive in cultivating a successful vegetable garden. We truly hope you'll discover the joy and satisfaction that comes from cultivating a thriving, harmonious vegetable garden and would love to share this experience with you via our Facebook gardening community - **facebook.com/groups/greenroots/**

Now that you're well-equipped to start your winter gardening journey, we would appreciate if you could give an honest review of this guide. Your feedback and thoughts help us determine whether we did an excellent job of assisting you in improving your gardening skills. Feel free to post them in the comments and reviews section of your purchased retailer, and we'll keep an eye out for them.

"Garden is not just a hobby, but a way of life" - Green Roots

ALSO BY GREEN ROOTS

Fruit and Veggies 101 - Vegetable Companion Planting: Companion Guide On How To Grow Vegetables Using Essential, Organic & Sustainable Gardening Strategies

Fruit and
Veggies 101

VEGETABLE COMPANION PLANTING

Companion Guide On How To Grow Vegetables Using Essential Organic & Sustainable Gardening Strategies

(Perfect For Beginners)

GREEN ROOTS

Fruit & Veggies 101 - Salad Vegetables: Gardening Guide On How To Grow the Freshest & Ripest Salad Vegetables (Perfect for Beginners)

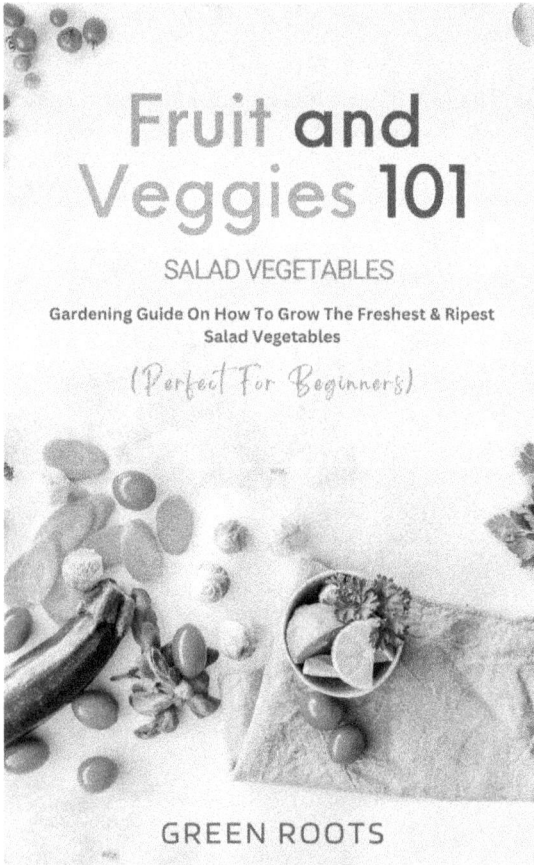

Fruit **and** Veggies **101**

SALAD VEGETABLES

Gardening Guide On How To Grow The Freshest & Ripest Salad Vegetables

(Perfect For Beginners)

GREEN ROOTS

Fruit & Veggies 101 - Summer Fruits: Gardening Guide on How to Grow the Freshest & Ripest Summer Fruits (Perfect for Beginners)

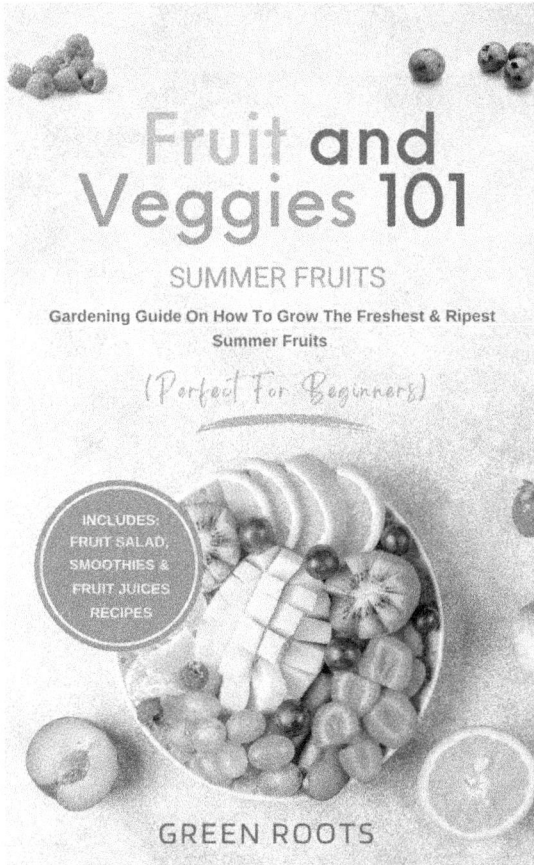

Fruit and Veggies 101

SUMMER FRUITS

Gardening Guide On How To Grow The Freshest & Ripest Summer Fruits

(Perfect For Beginners)

INCLUDES: FRUIT SALAD, SMOOTHIES & FRUIT JUICES RECIPES

GREEN ROOTS

BIBLIOGRAPHY

10 Reasons to Grow Your Own Organic Food. (2016, February 2). Grow a Good Life. https://growagoodlife.com/grow-your-own-organic-food/

Andrew. (2020, April 23). *What Tools Do I Need To Start a Vegetable Garden? - Gardening FAQs*. Quickcrop Blog. https://www.quickcrop.co.uk/blog/what-tools-do-i-need-to-start-a-vegetable-garden/

Asher, B. (2011). *What Is the Best Fertilizer for Cucumbers? | Hunker*. Hunker. https://www.hunker.com/13427375/what-is-the-best-fertilizer-for-cucumbers

Bailey, V. (2018, December 15). *What Not to Plant Near Cucumbers*. Home Guides | SF Gate. https://homeguides.sfgate.com/not-plant-near-cucumbers-33318.html

Balogh, A. (n.d.). *Garden Soil: How to Prepare Your Soil for a Garden - Garden Design*. GardenDesign.com. Retrieved June 27, 2021, from https://www.gardendesign.com/soil/

Benefits of Community Growing. (n.d.). Www.edibleestates.co.uk. http://www.edibleestates.co.uk/benefits-of-community-growing/

Blando, M. (n.d.). *How Much Sun Does a Cucumber Plant Need?* Homeguides.sfgate.com. https://homeguides.sfgate.com/much-sun-cucumber-plant-need-52857.html

Boeckmann, C. (2021, March 25). *Vegetable Gardening for Beginners*. Old Farmer's Almanac. https://www.almanac.com/vegetable-gardening-for-beginners

Borge, A. (2014, April 24). *The Financial Benefits of Starting a Vegetable Garden*. DebtHelper.com. https://debthelper.com/blog/2014/04/financial-benefits-starting-vegetable-garden/

Campbell-Preston, C. (2016, September 12). *Why Gardening is Great For Your Mental Health and Wellbeing | Capital Gardens*. Capital Gardens. https://www.capitalgardens.co.uk/blog/gardening-great-mental-health-wellbeing/

Castillo, E. (2016, May 7). *How much salad should you be eating each day?* PCOSbites. https://pcosbites.com/2016/05/07/how-much-salad-should-you-be-eating-each-day/

Domoney, D. (2019a, March 8). *Expert guide to soil*. David Domoney. https://www.daviddomoney.com/expert-guide-to-soil/

Domoney, D. (2019b, March 11). *Beginner's Guide to Growing Fruit and Veg*.

David Domoney. https://www.daviddomoney.com/beginners-guide-to-growing-fruit-and-veg/

Domoney, D. (2019c, May 13). *Benefits of Gardening for Mental Health*. David Domoney. https://www.daviddomoney.com/benefits-gardening-mental-health/

Druff, K. V. (2021, February 28). *8 Amazing Social Benefits of Gardening*. Bunny's Garden. https://www.bunnysgarden.com/social-benefits-of-gardening/

Ferrandino, F. (2014, April 25). *How to Prune Tomatoes*. FineGardening. https://www.finegardening.com/article/pruning-tomatoes

Gardening: Invest in guaranteed growth in your own backyard. (2009, April). Cappersfarmer.com. https://www.cappersfarmer.com/yard-and-garden/gardening-invest-in-guaranteed-growth-in-your-own-backyard/

George, H. (2020, August 29). *Identify, Prevent, and Treat Common Cabbage Diseases | Gardener's Path*. Gardener's Path. https://gardenerspath.com/how-to/disease-and-pests/common-cabbage-diseases/

Gibson, A. (2012, November 27). *Guide to Growing Spring Onions: Everything you need to know!* The Micro Gardener. https://themicrogardener.com/guide-to-growing-spring-onions/

Gillihan, S. J. (2019, June 19). *10 Mental Health Benefits of Gardening | Psychology Today United Kingdom*. Www.psychologytoday.com. https://www.psychologytoday.com/gb/blog/think-act-be/201906/10-mental-health-benefits-gardening

Go, G. (2014). *7 Surprising Financial Benefits of Gardening*. US News & World Report; U.S. News & World Report. https://money.usnews.com/money/blogs/my-money/2014/05/07/7-surprising-financial-benefits-of-gardening

Growing Cabbages & General Cabbage Planting Tips. (n.d.). Bonnie Plants. https://bonnieplants.com/how-to-grow/growing-cabbage/#:~:text=Like%20most%20vegetables%2C%20cabbage%20needs

Hagen, L. (2019). *12 Gardening Tools to Buy - Essentials for Beginners - Garden Design*. GardenDesign.com. https://www.gardendesign.com/how-to/tools.html

Haifa Group. (2018, March 11). *Crop Guide: Tomato*. Haifa Group. https://www.haifa-group.com/tomato-fertilizer/crop-guide-tomato

Hansen, J. (n.d.). *The Easiest Fruits and Vegetables to Grow for Beginners*. GardenTech.com. Retrieved July 11, 2021, from https://www.gardentech.com/blog/gardening-and-healthy-living/8-easy-to-grow-fruits-and-veggies

Harvard Health Publishing. (2018, August 13). *Calories burned in 30 minutes for people of three different weights - Harvard Health*. Harvard Health; Harvard Health. https://www.health.harvard.edu/diet-and-weight-loss/calories-burned-in-30-minutes-of-leisure-and-routine-activities

Hayes, K. (2017, June 14). *5 Health Benefits of Gardening and Planting*. AARP. https://www.aarp.org/health/healthy-living/info-2017/health-benefits-of-gardening-fd.html

Heirloom Organics. (n.d.-a). *How to Grow Cucumbers | Guide to Growing Cucumbers*. Www.heirloom-Organics.com. Retrieved July 18, 2021, from http://www.heirloom-organics.com/guide/va/guidetogrowingcucumbers.html

Heirloom Organics. (n.d.-b). *How to Grow Tomato | Guide to Growing Tomatoes*. Www.heirloom-Organics.com. Retrieved July 17, 2021, from http://www.heirloom-organics.com/guide/va/guidetogrowingtomato.html

How to Grow Cabbage | Guide to Growing Cabbage. (n.d.). Www.heirloom-Organics.com. Retrieved August 2, 2021, from http://www.heirloom-organics.com/guide/va/guidetogrowingcabbage.html

How to Grow Carrots | Guide to Growing Carrots. (n.d.). Www.heirloom-Organics.com. Retrieved August 5, 2021, from http://www.heirloom-organics.com/guide/va/guidetogrowingcarrots.html

How to Grow Pepper | Guide to Growing Peppers. (n.d.). Www.heirloom-Organics.com. Retrieved August 5, 2021, from http://www.heirloom-organics.com/guide/va/guidetogrowingpeppers.html

How to Grow Radishes - Gardening Tips and Advice, Vegetable Seeds and Plants at Burpee.com. (2019). Burpee.com. https://www.burpee.com/gardenadvicecenter/vegetables/radishes/all-about-radishes/article10099.html

How to Grow Radishes | Guide to Growing Radishes. (n.d.). Www.heirloom-Organics.com. Retrieved August 5, 2021, from http://www.heirloom-organics.com/guide/va/guidetogrowingradish.html

Hutchins, R. (2017, October 31). *8 Surprising Health Benefits of Gardening | UNC Health Talk*. UNC Health Talk. https://healthtalk.unchealthcare.org/health-benefits-of-gardening/

KJ Staff. (2020, November 25). *What are the Different Methods of Sowing Seeds?* Krishijagran.com. https://krishijagran.com/agripedia/what-are-the-different-methods-of-sowing-seeds/

Knerl, L. (2021, July 24). *The True Cost Of Growing A Garden*. Investopedia. https://www.investopedia.com/financial-edge/0312/the-true-cost-of-growing-a-garden.aspx

Larum, D. (2021, January 13). *StackPath*. Www.gardeningknowhow.com. https://www.gardeningknowhow.com/edible/vegetables/tomato/protecting-tomatoes-from-animals.htm

Leichty, C. (n.d.). *Are Raised Garden Beds Better than In-Ground Garden Beds?* Do Not Disturb Gardening. Retrieved June 26, 2021, from https://donot-disturbgardening.com/are-raised-garden-beds-better-than-in-ground-garden-beds/

Lobo, B. (2021, March 28). *Growing Tomatoes From Seed: How, When and Ideal Temperatures.* Dengarden - Home and Garden. https://dengarden.com/gardening/planting-tomato-seeds

Loek, Z. (2020, January 31). *Every Gardener Needs A Good Rake And Hoe.* Hobby Farms. https://www.hobbyfarms.com/every-gardener-needs-a-good-rake-and-hoe/

Lussier, M. (2018, May 30). *5 Reasons To Grow Your Own Food.* Healthy UNH. https://www.unh.edu/healthyunh/blog/nutrition/2018/05/5-reasons-grow-your-own-food

Maggie's Farm. (2020, May 20). *Common Tomato Insects and How to Protect Your Plants.* Maggie's Farm. https://maggiesfarmproducts.com/blogs/bug-help/tomato-pests

Mantel, S. (2019). *Why are soils important?* | *ISRIC.* Isric.org. https://www.isric.org/discover/about_soils/why-are-soils-important

Masley, S. (2019, October 4). *How to Prepare the Soil for a Vegetable Garden.* WikiHow. https://www.wikihow.com/Prepare-the-Soil-for-a-Vegetable-Garden

Max. (2020, July 5). *15 Different Types of Cucumbers That You Can Grow.* Trees.com. https://www.trees.com/edible/cucumbers

Newcomb, L. (n.d.). *Remedy for Nitrogen Overdose on Tomato Plants.* Home Guides | SF Gate. https://homeguides.sfgate.com/remedy-nitrogen-overdose-tomato-plants-29733.html

Old Farmer's Almanac. (2017, August 12). *Soil pH Levels for Plants.* Old Farmer's Almanac. https://www.almanac.com/plant-ph

Old Farmer's Almanac. (2019, July 4). *Radishes.* Old Farmer's Almanac. https://www.almanac.com/plant/radishes

Palomo, E. (n.d.). *Do Cucumbers Have Shallow Roots?* Home Guides | SF Gate. Retrieved July 18, 2021, from https://homeguides.sfgate.com/cucumbers-shallow-roots-85473.html

Paul. (n.d.). *Different types of gardens.* Www.clausehomegarden.com. Retrieved June 26, 2021, from https://www.clausehomegarden.com/rubrique-concept/resistances-aux-maladies/different-types-gardens

Pleasant, B. (2019, March 14). *8 Tips for Growing Tomatoes from Seed.* GrowVeg. https://www.growveg.co.uk/guides/8-tips-for-growing-tomatoes-from-seed/

Quinn, L. (2016, April 26). *The Benefits of Growing a Vegetable Garden.* Burke

Rehabilitation Hospital. https://www.burke.org/blog/2016/4/the-benefits-of-growing-a-vegetable-garden/83

Reilly, K. (2020, April 15). *The Only Tools You Need to Start a Garden*. Eating-Well. https://www.eatingwell.com/article/17068/the-only-tools-you-need-to-start-a-garden/

Rhoades, H. (2021a, June 4). *StackPath*. Www.gardeningknowhow.com. https://www.gardeningknowhow.com/edible/vegetables/tomato/watering-tomato-plants.htm

Rhoades, H. (2021b, June 29). *StackPath*. Www.gardeningknowhow.com. https://www.gardeningknowhow.com/edible/vegetables/tomato/tomato-fertilizer.htm

Sanderson, S. (n.d.). *How To Grow Tomatoes | Thompson & Morgan*. Www.thompson-Morgan.com. Retrieved July 17, 2021, from https://www.thompson-morgan.com/how-to-grow-tomatoes

SCOTT, T. L., MASSER, B. M., & PACHANA, N. A. (2014). Exploring the health and wellbeing benefits of gardening for older adults. *Ageing and Society*, 35(10), 2176–2200. https://doi.org/10.1017/s0144686x14000865

Search | Garden Organic. (2016, February 9). Www.gardenorganic.org.uk. http://www.gardenorganic.org.uk/sites/www.gardenorganic.org.uk/

Sedghi, S. (2019, May 16). *10 Common Types of Tomatoes—and What to Do With Them*. MyRecipes. https://www.myrecipes.com/ingredients/types-of-tomatoes

Sherry, D. (2014, April 25). *How to Harvest Tomatoes*. FineGardening. https://www.finegardening.com/article/how-to-harvest-tomatoes

Sigler, J. (2009a, March 24). *A Beginner's Guide to Fruit and Vegetable Gardening*. SparkPeople. https://www.sparkpeople.com/resource/nutrition_articles.asp?id=1292

Sigler, J. (2009b, March 24). *A Beginner's Guide to Fruit and Vegetable Gardening*. SparkPeople. https://www.sparkpeople.com/resource/nutrition_articles.asp?id=1292

Simons, L. A., Simons, J., McCallum, J., & Friedlander, Y. (2006). Lifestyle factors and risk of dementia: Dubbo Study of the elderly. *Medical Journal of Australia*, 184(2), 68–70. https://doi.org/10.5694/j.1326-5377.2006.tb00120.x

Singh, B. (2021, March 23). *Sowing - An Overview and Different Methods of Sowing Seeds*. BYJUS. https://byjus.com/biology/sowing/

Smith, C. (n.d.). *Tomato Root Rot Due to Rain*. Home Guides | SF Gate. Retrieved July 18, 2021, from https://homeguides.sfgate.com/tomato-root-rot-due-rain-27887.html

Sowing, different types of sowing. (2017, July 28). Nature and Garden. https://www.nature-and-garden.com/gardening/sowing.html#

Stanborough, R. (2020, June 17). *10 Benefits of Gardening, Plus Helpful Tips & Recommendations.* Healthline. https://www.healthline.com/health/healthful-benefits-of-gardening#takeaway

Stross, A. (2016, January 28). *How to Start a Garden on a Budget.* Tenth Acre Farm. https://www.tenthacrefarm.com/how-to-start-a-garden-on-a-budget/

The benefits of gardening and food growing for health and wellbeing | Sustain. (2014, April 1). Www.sustainweb.org. https://www.sustainweb.org/publications/the_benefits_of_gardening_and_food_growing/

The Royal Horticultural Society. (2020). *How to grow tomatoes | RHS Gardening.* Rhs.org.uk; Royal Horticultural Society. https://www.rhs.org.uk/advice/grow-your-own/vegetables/tomatoes

The therapeutic properties of growing and gardening | Garden Organic. (n.d.). Www.gardenorganic.org.uk. Retrieved August 5, 2021, from https://www.gardenorganic.org.uk/therapeutic-properties-growing-and-gardening#:~:text=Mental%20health%20and%20well%2Dbeing

Thomas, C. (2021, June 29). *Save Money By Growing Your Own Veg.* Which? https://www.which.co.uk/reviews/grow-your-own/article/growing-vegetables/save-money-by-growing-your-own-veg-a8zgZ4G3O3AC

Tilley, N. (2021, July 27). *StackPath.* Www.gardeningknowhow.com. https://www.gardeningknowhow.com/edible/vegetables/cucumber/when-to-pick-a-cucumber-how-to-prevent-yellow-cucumbers.htm

Unusual Urban Planting: 5 Different Types of Gardening. (2008, July 9). WebUrbanist. https://weburbanist.com/2008/07/09/5-different-types-of-gardening-unconventional-and-conventional-urban-planting/

Vinje, E. (2012, December 8). *Beginner Tomato Gardening Guide.* Planet Natural. https://www.planetnatural.com/tomato-gardening/

www.ingramcontent.com/pod-product-compliance
Lightning Source LLC
Chambersburg PA
CBHW051828040426
42447CB00006B/425